GREAT TASTES

PASTA

First published in 2009 by Bay Books, an imprint of Murdoch Books Pty Limited
This edition published in 2010.

Murdoch Books Australia
Pier 8/9
23 Hickson Road
Millers Point NSW 2000
Phone: +61 (0) 2 8220 2000
Fax: +61 (0) 2 8220 2558
www.murdochbooks.com.au

Murdoch Books UK Limited
Erico House, 6th Floor
93–99 Upper Richmond Road
Putney, London SW15 2TG
Phone: +44 (0) 20 8785 5995
Fax: +44 (0) 20 8785 5985
www.murdochbooks.co.uk

Chief Executive: Juliet Rogers
Publishing Director: Kay Scarlett
Publisher: Lynn Lewis
Senior Designer: Heather Menzies
Designer: Wendy Inkster
Production: Kita George
Index: Jo Rudd

ISBN: 9781741965827

PRINTED IN CHINA

IMPORTANT: Those who might be at risk from the effects of salmonella poisoning (the elderly, pregnant women, young children and those suffering from immune deficiency diseases) should consult their doctor with any concerns about eating raw eggs.

OVEN GUIDE: You may find cooking times vary depending on the oven you are using. For fan-forced ovens, as a general rule, set the oven temperature to 20°C (35°F) lower than indicated in the recipe.

GREAT TASTES
PASTA

More than 120 easy recipes for every day

bay books

CONTENTS

PASTA BASICS

Pasta can be as simple or as extravagant as you like — depending upon its accompanying sauce. Most pasta dishes are enhanced by the addition of cheese. Pasta, cheese and salad makes a well-balanced and delicious meal.

How to cook pasta

Use a very large pan of water. For 500 g of pasta you will need at least 4 litres of water. Bring water, salted if desired, to a rapid boil and add pasta gradually so that the water continues to boil. The pasta should be able to move freely to prevent it sticking together. Stir occasionally with a long-handled fork or spoon to prevent pasta sticking to bottom of the pan.

Long pasta such as spaghetti should be eased into the water rather than broken. Hold one end and put the other end in the boiling water. As pasta softens, gently lower it into the water until it is all immersed. Make sure the water boils rapidly while pasta is cooking. Do not cover pan.

Some people like to add a few drops of olive oil to the water to help prevent sticking.

Timing of pasta cooking is very important. Follow the directions on the packet and before stated time is up, remove a piece and test it. It should be at the point of still firm but just tender (al dente). Dried pasta usually takes 8–12 minutes and fresh pasta about 3–6 minutes, depending on the size and thickness. Drain pasta into a colander as soon as it is ready.

Pasta is best used as soon as it is cooked but if you have to keep it warm for a while, drain and toss with a little olive oil to keep pieces separate. If it is to be used cold in a salad rinse thoroughly under cold water after cooking. Drain and toss in a little oil. Refrigerate.

The recipes in this book use dried pasta unless fresh pasta is specified. If you prefer, you can substitute fresh. Vary the cooking time accordingly.

AMOUNT OF PASTA PER PERSON: For an average serving, you will need 75–125 g (3–5 oz) of dried pasta per person and 125–175 g (5–7 oz) of fresh pasta.

TO SERVE: The traditional way of serving pasta such as spaghetti or fettucine is to divide cooked pasta into individual serving bowls and toss with a little of the sauce. The remaining sauce is then placed in a bowl at the table so guests can help themselves.

An easy way to serve is to return drained, cooked pasta to pan. Add sauce; toss until combined. Transfer to large serving bowl or divide between individual serving dishes.

Long pasta

There is an enormous variety of widths, thicknesses and shapes of long pasta. Round ones include spaghetti, vermicelli and spaghettini. Some, such as bucatini, have a hole through the middle to allow thin sauces to flow through.

Spaghetti is often served simply with oil and garlic. However, it can be served with any sauce which clings to the pasta. Vermicelli can be used in the same way. Flat, long pasta such as fettucine, tagliatelle and linguine are also best with sauces which cling when strands are picked up.

Seafood, is often served with long pasta but big, chunky pieces of vegetables and meat aren't easy to eat with any of the long pasta. Bolognaise sauce goes well with spaghetti and tagliatelle.

TO EAT: Use a fork to spear a few strands and place the tip of the fork against a spoon. Twirl fork so strands wind around the fork. Or just push the fork against the plate and twirl.

Short pasta

These are straight or shaped and sometimes tubular. Tubular and shaped short pasta retain the accompanying sauce well and are easy to pick up with most sauces, including chunky meat and vegetables. All short pastas are interchangeable.

Dried pasta is commercially prepared and packaged, made from flour, water and salt and sometimes egg. Some shapes are especially suited to a particular type of sauce.

Fresh pasta is now available from supermarkets and delicatessens. Some are flavoured with herbs and spices or coloured with vegetables. Fresh pasta cooks a lot more quickly than dried pasta.

CONCHIGLIE: Shell-shaped pasta which comes in various sizes. Large shells are excellent for baking with fillings such as seafood whereas small shells can be used in casseroles and soups or can be served cold in salads.

FARFALLE: Butterfly- or bow tie- shaped pasta. Excellent with meat or vegetable sauces.

FUSILLI: Twist or spiral pasta—good in salads and with meat sauces as the meat gets caught in the spirals.

MACARONI: Straight or curved (elbows) short lengths of pasta with a hole through the centre. Often used in baked dishes.

PENNE: Straight short lengths with a smooth or ridged surface, with a wide hole through the middle. Ends are cut at an angle. Retain sauce well.

LASAGNE SHEETS: Flat or ridged sheets of pasta. Layered with sauces and then baked. Some need pre-cooking before layering. Follow the manufacturer's instructions.

Filled pasta

CANNELLONI TUBES: Pasta shape with a hole big enough for filling with meat and vegetable sauces. After filling, they are baked with a sauce poured over the top to keep them moist.

RAVIOLI AND TORTELLINI: Pasta shapes with a variety of fillings including vegetable, chicken and meat. Buy them fresh or dried or make your own. They are cooked separately and usually served with mild sauces that don't overwhelm the flavour of the filling.

Gnocchi

Small savoury dumplings made with vegetables or semolina. They are poached and served with sauces.

Pasta for soups

Many different shapes are available for adding to soups and casseroles. There are little stars (stelline), small versions of shells (conchiglie) and farfalle (butterflies or bow ties) and even pasta in the shape of letters of the alphabet.

Use a vegetable peeler to shave fresh parmesan very thinly for garnishes and salads.

Cheese

Cheese, most commonly parmesan, is often used in pasta dishes. Sometimes it is part of the sauce, sometimes simply used as a garnish. Cheese used in pasta dishes should be freshly grated — avoid ready-grated cheeses.

For storage, it is preferable that hard cheeses be wrapped tightly in foil or kitchen paper and refrigerated. If you prefer to use plastic wrap, squeeze out as much air as possible and then wrap in foil as well.

PARMESAN: Is a hard granular, light yellow cheese with a very strong flavour which blends extremely well with meat, tomato and vegetable sauces as well as some creamy sauces and soups. parmesan cheese keeps for months if wrapped tightly before refrigeration.

PARMIGIANO-REGGIANO: Is the best type of parmesan with a good strong flavour. The rind should have its name marked on it.

GRUYÈRE: Is a form of firm Swiss cheese, pale yellow in colour. gruyère varies from dry and strong-flavoured to a more mild creamy style. The creamy one is preferable in most sauces. gruyère is an excellent melting cheese which draws hardly any threads. You can use a cheddar as a substitute if you prefer.

ROMANO: Is a hard granular cheese with a biting flavour. It has small holes throughout and is golden yellow, darkening with maturity. Sometimes it is used as a substitute for parmesan cheese. Like parmesan, it is often finely grated or shaved for use as a garnish to enhance the flavour of pasta dishes.

PECORINO: Is a hard granular cheese, pale yellow, darkening with maturity. It has a stronger, more piquant, tangy taste than parmesan and can be used as a substitute for parmesan if you enjoy the biting flavour. Like parmesan, it stores for a long time.

RICOTTA: Is a moist, fine, white cheese with a sweet, delicate flavour. The texture is quite creamy. It is very good for use in the fillings for pasta dishes such as cannelloni and is quite often used in the cooking of sweet dishes.

BOCCONCINI AND OVOLINI: Are soft, moist, mild, almost white cheeses. Ovolini is a small version of bocconcini. If bought unpackaged from delicatessens, refrigerate in the whey that they come in and use within 3 days.

MOZZARELLA: Is a soft, smooth cheese, pale yellow in colour. It has a mild, sweet flavour and is excellent for recipes that have the cheese melted on top and for use in salads.

GORGONZOLA: Is a soft, creamy, blue-veined cheese with quite a pungent smell and a strong bite to its taste. It adds richness to pasta dishes but you can choose a milder-flavoured blue cheese, if you prefer a more subtle taste.

CHEDDAR: Comes in various strengths including mild, semi-matured, matured and vintage. They are all quite firm but the more mature ones are often more crumbly.

BASIC SAUCES

TOMATO SAUCE
Serves 4–6

1.5 kg (3 lb 6 oz) large ripe tomatoes

1 tablespoon olive oil

2 garlic cloves, crushed

1 onion, chopped

1 medium carrot, finely chopped

2 tablespoons tomato paste

1 teaspoon sugar

salt and pepper, to taste

60 g (2 oz/¼ cup) freshly chopped mixed oregano, parsley and basil

500 g (1 lb 2 oz) rigatoni, penne, spaghetti or pasta of your choice

1   Mark a small cross in the top of each tomato. Place the tomatoes in boiling water for 1–2 minutes, then plunge into cold water. Remove and peel skin down from the cross. Discard the skin and roughly chop the tomatoes.

2   Heat the oil in heavy-based pan. Add the garlic and onion and cook for 5 minutes over low heat.

3   Add the tomatoes and carrot, cook, stirring occasionally, for 10 minutes. Add the tomato paste, sugar, salt and pepper. Bring to boil and cook a further 2 minutes.

4   Place the sauce mixture in a food processor and process briefly until sauce reaches desired consistency. Add herbs and stir to combine.

5   While sauce is cooking, add the pasta to a large pan of rapidly boiling water and cook until just tender. Drain and return to pan. Add the sauce to pasta and toss well to combine.

Note: Sauce may be stored, covered, in the refrigerator for up to 3 days or frozen for up to 3 months.

GARLIC SAUCE WITH PARSLEY
Serves 4–6

4 garlic cloves

500 g (1 lb 2 oz) fusilli or spiral pasta

250 ml (8 fl oz/1 cup) olive oil

60 g (2 oz/¼ cup) chopped parsley

salt and pepper, to taste

1   Crush or finely chop the garlic into small bowl.

2   Add the pasta to a large pan of boiling water and cook until just tender. Drain the pasta and return to the pan.

3   About five minutes before the pasta is cooked, heat the oil in heavy-based pan over a low heat. Add the garlic to pan and cook for 30 seconds or until garlic is soft.

4   Pour the oil and garlic over the hot pasta. Add the chopped parsley, salt and pepper and toss until the pasta is well coated. Serve immediately.

Note: Cook the garlic until golden brown but not any darker as it will turn bitter. Buy fresh plump garlic, not old, dried out bulbs. Variations: Add 1 cup chopped olives with the parsley. Add 2 tablespoons of chopped fresh oregano, basil, chives or sage with the parsley. Add 4 chopped anchovies when cooking the garlic.

PESTO SAUCE
Serves 4–6

500 g (1 lb) tagliatelle or fettucine

40 g (1½ oz/¼ cup) pine nuts

100 g (4 oz/2 cups) basil leaves

2 garlic cloves, crushed

½ teaspoon salt

30 g (1 oz/¼ cup) freshly grated parmesan cheese

2 tablespoons freshly grated pecorino cheese (optional)

125 ml (4 fl oz/½ cup) olive oil

black pepper, to taste

1   Add the pasta to a large pan of rapidly boiling water and cook until just tender. Drain and return to the pan.

2   About 5 minutes before the pasta is cooked, add the pine nuts to a heavy-based pan and stir over a low heat for 2–3 minutes or until golden. Cool.

3   Place the pine nuts, basil leaves, garlic and salt in food processor and process for 10 seconds. Scrape down the sides of the bowl.

4   Add the cheeses, process for another 10 seconds. With motor running, gradually add the oil until a paste is formed. Add the pepper.

5   Add the pesto to warm pasta and toss until sauce coats pasta.

Note: Pesto sauce can be made up to 1 week in advance and stored in an airtight container in the refrigerator.

1 **Heat the oil** in a large deep pan. Add the garlic, onion, carrot and celery. Cook, stirring, for 5 minutes over a low heat until golden.

2 **Increase the heat** and add the mince, breaking it up with a fork as it cooks. Stir until well browned.

3 **Add the stock,** wine, undrained, crushed tomatoes, sugar and parsley. Bring to the boil, then reduce the heat and simmer uncovered for 1½ hours, stirring occasionally.

4 **Add salt and pepper,** to taste. Before the sauce has finished cooking, add the pasta to a pan of rapidly boiling water and cook until just tender. Drain well.

5 **Serve the sauce** over the top of the pasta. Sprinkle with parmesan cheese.

Note: The bolognaise sauce can be used cold for layering in a lasagne. Make a day ahead and store, covered, in refrigerator.

BOLOGNAISE SAUCE
Serves 4–6

2 tablespoons olive oil

2 garlic cloves, crushed

1 large onion, chopped

1 medium carrot, chopped

1 stick celery, chopped

500 g (1 lb 2 oz) beef mince

500 ml (17 fl oz/2 cups) beef stock

750 ml (24 fl oz/1½ cups) red wine

2 x 425 g (14 oz) can tomatoes

1 teaspoon sugar

2 tablespoons chopped fresh parsley

salt and pepper, to taste

500 g (1 lb) spaghetti or tagliatelle

2 tablespoons freshly grated parmesan cheese, for serving

---

1 **Heat the oil** in a large deep pan. Add the onion, bacon and carrot and stir for 5 minutes over a medium heat.

2 **Add the mince,** breaking up any lumps with the back of a fork. Cook until the meat is well browned.

3 **Stir in the tomato paste,** undrained, crushed tomatoes and mixed herbs. Bring to the boil, then reduce heat and simmer, uncovered, for 15 minutes or until meat is tender. Add salt and pepper, to taste.

4 **While the sauce is cooking,** add the pasta to a large pan of boiling water and cook until just tender. Drain well.

5 **Serve the sauce** over the pasta. Sprinkle with parmesan cheese, if desired.

Note: If you don't like a strong herb taste, use chopped fresh herbs of your choice — use about 2 tablespoons.

25 MINUTE BOLOGNAISE SAUCE
Serves 4–6

1 tablespoon olive oil

1 medium onion, chopped

2 rashers bacon, chopped

1 medium carrot, grated

750 g (1 lb 10 oz) beef mince

100 g (4 oz/½ cup) tomato paste

425 g (14 oz) can tomatoes

1 teaspoon dried mixed herbs

salt and pepper, to taste

500 g (1 lb) spaghetti or tagliatelle

SOUPS
& SALADS

HEARTY ITALIAN BEAN AND PASTA SOUP

SERVES 4

1 tablespoon olive oil

1 onion, finely chopped

3 garlic cloves, crushed

2 x 300 g (10 oz) tins mixed beans, drained

1.75 litres (60 fl oz/6½ cups) chicken stock (see Note)

100 g (3½ oz) conchigliette

1 tablespoon chopped fresh tarragon

1   Heat the oil in a saucepan over low heat. Add the onion and cook for 5 minutes, then add the garlic and cook for a further 1 minute, stirring frequently. Add the beans and chicken stock and then cover the pan with a lid.

2   Increase the heat and bring to the boil. Add the pasta and cook until just tender.

3   Stir in the tarragon, then season with salt and freshly cracked black pepper. Serve with crusty bread.

Note: The flavour of this soup is really enhanced by using a good-quality stock. Either make your own or use the tetra packs of liquid stock that are available at the supermarket.

WARM PESTO PASTA SALAD

SERVES 4

pesto (see recipe on page 8), or ready-made

500 g (1 lb 2 oz) orecchiette or shell pasta

2 tablespoons olive oil

150 g (5 oz) jar capers, drained and patted dry

2 tablespoons extra virgin olive oil

2 garlic cloves, chopped

3 tomatoes, seeded and diced

300 g (10 oz) thin asparagus spears, cut in half and blanched

2 tablespoons balsamic vinegar

200 g (6½ oz) rocket (arugula), trimmed and cut into short lengths

parmesan shavings, to garnish

1 **Make the pesto** – see recipe on page 8.

2 **Cook the pasta** in a large saucepan of boiling water until just tender, then drain well.

3 **Meanwhile**, heat the oil in a frying pan, add the capers and fry over high heat, stirring occasionally, for 4–5 minutes, or until crisp. Remove from the pan and drain on crumpled paper towels.

4 **In the same frying pan,** heat the extra virgin olive oil over medium heat and add the garlic, tomato and asparagus. Cook for 1–2 minutes, or until warmed through, tossing well. Stir in the balsamic vinegar.

5 **Drain the pasta** and transfer to a large serving bowl. Add the pesto and toss, coating the pasta well. Cool slightly. Add the tomato mixture and rocket and season to taste with salt and cracked black pepper. Toss well and sprinkle with the capers and parmesan. Serve warm.

SWEET POTATO, ROCKET AND WALNUT PASTA SALAD

SERVES 4

800 g (1 lb 12 oz) orange sweet potato,
  cut into 2 cm (¾ inch) cubes

150 ml (5 fl oz) olive oil

125 g (4½ oz/1 cup) walnut pieces

350 g (12 oz) fricelli

150 g (5½ oz) white castello cheese,
  softened

2 garlic cloves, crushed

2 teaspoons lemon juice

½ teaspoon sugar

100 g (3½ oz) baby rocket (arugula)

1   Preheat the oven to 200°C (400°F/Gas 6). Toss the orange sweet potato in 2 tablespoons of the oil and place in a single layer on a baking tray lined with baking paper. Season. Roast, turning halfway through, for 30 minutes, or until golden and cooked through.

2   Spread the walnuts on a baking tray and roast for 10 minutes, or until crisp.

3   Meanwhile, cook the pasta in a large saucepan of boiling salted water until al dente. Drain well and return to the pan to keep warm.

4   Remove the rind from one-third of the cheese and cut the rest into cubes.

5   Finely chop 2 tablespoons of the walnuts. Combine with the garlic, lemon juice, sugar, remaining oil and rindless cheese. Season.

6   Combine the pasta, sweet potato, rocket, cubed cheese and remaining walnuts in a bowl. Drizzle with the dressing and toss together. Season.

TOMATO DITALINI SOUP

SERVES 4–6

2 tablespoons olive oil

1 large onion, finely chopped

2 celery stalks, finely chopped

3 vine-ripened tomatoes

1.5 litres (52 fl oz/6 cups) vegetable stock

90 g (3 oz/½ cup) ditalini pasta

2 tablespoons chopped fresh flat-leaf (Italian) parsley

crusty bread, to serve

1 **Heat the oil** in a large saucepan over medium heat. Add the onion and celery and cook for 5 minutes, or until they have softened.

2 **Score a cross** in the base of each tomato, then place them in a bowl of boiling water for 1 minute. Plunge into cold water and peel the skin away from the cross. Halve the tomatoes and scoop out the seeds. Roughly chop the flesh.

3 **Add the stock** and tomato to the onion mixture and bring to the boil.

4 **Add the pasta** and cook for 10 minutes, or until just tender. Season. Sprinkle with parsley. Serve with crusty bread.

BACON AND PEA SOUP

SERVES 4–6

1 large onion

4 rashers bacon

60 g (2 oz) butter

1 stick celery, chopped into small pieces

2 litres (70 fl oz/8 cups) chicken stock

155 g (5 oz/1 cup) frozen green peas

250 g (8 oz) risoni

2 tablespoons chopped fresh parsley

pepper, to taste

1 **Peel the onion** and chop finely. Trim the rind and excess fat from bacon and chop into small pieces.

2 **Place bacon,** butter, onion and celery in large heavy-based pan. Cook for 5 minutes over a low heat, stirring occasionally.

3 **Add chicken stock** and peas and simmer, covered for 5 minutes. Increase heat and add the pasta; cook, uncovered, stirring occasionally, for 5 minutes, or until pasta is tender.

4 **Add the chopped parsley** and pepper just before serving.

Note: You can make this soup the day before required and store in an airtight container in refrigerator. Gently reheat before serving. Double-smoked bacon will give the best flavour.

SPAGHETTI TOMATO SALAD

SERVES 4–6

500 g (1 lb 2 oz) spaghettini or spaghetti

50 g (2 oz/1 cup) fresh basil leaves

250 g (8 oz) cherry tomatoes, halved

1 clove garlic, crushed

75 g (3 oz/½ cup) chopped black olives

60 ml (2 fl oz/¼ cup) olive oil

1 tablespoon balsamic vinegar

60 g (2 oz/½ cup) freshly grated
    parmesan cheese

salt and pepper, to taste

1 **Add the pasta** to a large pan of rapidly boiling water and cook until just tender. Drain the pasta and rinse well under cold water.

2 **Using a sharp knife,** chop basil leaves into fine strips.

3 **In a bowl combine the basil,** tomato, garlic, olives, oil and vinegar. Allow to stand for 15 minutes. Place the drained pasta in a large salad bowl and add the tomato mixture.

4 **Add the parmesan,** salt and pepper. Toss well and serve immediately.

Note: Pasta can be cooked up to 1 day in advance. If doing this, cool pasta and toss with a little oil.

FARFALLE SALAD WITH SUN-DRIED TOMATOES

SERVES 4–6

500 g (1 lb 2 oz) farfalle (butterfly pasta) or spiral pasta

3 spring onions

60 g (2 oz) sundried (sun-blushed) tomatoes, cut into strips

1 bunch English spinach, stalks trimmed and leaves shredded

40 g (1½ oz/¼ cup) toasted pine nuts

1 tablespoon chopped fresh oregano

DRESSING

60 ml (2 fl oz/¼ cup) olive oil

1 teaspoon fresh chopped chilli

1 clove garlic, crushed

salt and pepper, to taste

1 **Add the pasta** to a large pan of rapidly boiling water and cook until just tender. Drain the pasta and rinse well under cold water. Transfer to a large salad bowl.

2 **Trim the spring onions** and chop finely. Add to the pasta along with tomato, spinach, pine nuts and oregano.

3 **To make the dressing,** combine the oil, chilli, garlic, salt and pepper in a small screwtop jar and shake well.

4 **Pour the dressing** over the top of salad; toss well and serve.

MINESTRONE

125 g (4 oz) dried borlotti beans

1 large onion, roughly chopped

2 garlic cloves

1 medium handful roughly chopped fresh flat-leaf (Italian) parsley

60 g (2 oz) pancetta, chopped

60 ml (2 fl oz/¼ cup) olive oil

1 celery stalk, halved lengthways, cut into 1 cm (½ inch) slices

1 carrot, halved lengthways, cut into 1 cm (½ inch) slices

1 potato, diced

2 teaspoons tomato paste (concentrated purée)

420 g (14 oz) tin chopped tomatoes

6 fresh basil leaves, roughly torn

2 litres (70 fl oz/8 cups) chicken or vegetable stock

2 thin zucchini (courgettes), cut into 1.5 cm (⅝ inch) slices

115 g (4 oz/¾ cup) shelled peas

60 g (2 oz) green beans, cut into 4 cm (1½ inch) lengths

90 g (3 oz) silverbeet leaves, shredded

75 g (2½ oz) ditalini or small pasta

pesto, for garnish (see recipe on page 8), or ready-made

1 Put the beans in a large bowl, cover with water and soak overnight. Drain and rinse under cold water.

2 Place the onion, garlic, parsley and pancetta in a food processor and process until finely chopped.

3 Heat the oil in a saucepan, add the pancetta mixture and cook over low heat, stirring occasionally, for 8–10 minutes.

4 Add the celery, carrot and potato, and cook for 5 minutes, then stir in the tomato paste, tomato, basil and borlotti beans. Season with black pepper.

5 Add the stock and bring slowly to the boil. Cover and simmer, stirring occasionally, for 1½ hours.

6 Season, and add the zucchini, peas, green beans, silverbeet and pasta. Simmer for 8–10 minutes, or until the vegetables and pasta are just tender.

7 Transfer to a bowl and stir in the parmesan and freshly ground black pepper to taste. Serve the soup in bowls with dollops of pesto on top.

COUNTRY PUMPKIN AND PASTA SOUP

SERVES 4–6

1 large onion

about 700 g (1 lb 8 oz) pumpkin

2 medium potatoes

1 tablespoon olive oil

30 g (1 oz) butter

2 garlic cloves, crushed

3 litres (100 fl oz/12 cups) light chicken stock

125 g (4 oz) miniature pasta or risoni

1 tablespoon chopped fresh parsley, for serving, optional

1 **Peel the onion** and chop finely. Peel the pumpkin and potatoes and chop into small cubes.

2 **Heat the oil** and butter in a large pan. Add the onion and garlic and cook, stirring, for 5 minutes over low heat.

3 **Add the pumpkin,** potato and chicken stock. Increase the heat, cover the pan and cook for 8 minutes or until the vegetables are tender.

4 **Add the pasta** and cook, stirring occasionally, for about 5 minutes or until pasta is just tender.

5 **Serve immediately.** Sprinkle with chopped parsley, if desired.

Note: Butternut or Japanese pumpkin will give the sweetest flavour. Tiny star-shaped pasta look attractive in this soup.

SUCCULENT CHICKEN AND PASTA SALAD

SERVES 4

250 g (9 oz) boneless, skinless, chicken breast

375 ml (12 fl oz/1½ cups) chicken stock

350 g (12 oz) fusilli pasta

155 g (5½ oz) asparagus, cut into short lengths

150 g (5½ oz) gruyère cheese, grated

2 spring onions (scallions), thinly sliced

DRESSING

60 ml (2 fl oz/¼ cup) olive oil

60 ml (2 fl oz/¼ cup) lemon juice

½ teaspoon sugar

1 **Put the chicken** and stock in a frying pan. Bring to the boil, then reduce the heat and poach gently, turning regularly, for 8 minutes, or until tender. Remove the chicken, cool and slice thinly.

2 **Cook the pasta** in a large pan of boiling salted water for 10–12 minutes, or until just tender. Drain and cool.

3 **Cook the asparagus** in boiling water for 2 minutes. Drain and place in a bowl of iced water. Drain again.

4 **Combine with chicken,** pasta and cheese in a large bowl.

5 **To make the dressing,** whisk the ingredients together. Season with salt and pepper. Add to the salad and toss well.

6 **Transfer to a serving bowl.** Scatter with the spring onion.

WARM MINTED CHICKEN AND COTELLI SALAD

SERVES 4

250 g (9 oz) cotelli

125 ml (4 fl oz/½ cup) olive oil

1 large red capsicum (pepper)

3 boneless, skinless chicken breasts

6 spring onions (scallions), cut into 2 cm (¾ inch) lengths

4 garlic cloves, thinly sliced

3 large handfuls chopped mint

4 tablespoons cider vinegar

100 g (3½ oz/2 cups) baby English spinach leaves

1 Cook the pasta in a large saucepan of boiling salted water until just tender. Drain well and return to the pan to keep warm. Stir in 1 tablespoon of the oil.

2 Meanwhile, cut the capsicum into quarters and remove the membrane and seeds. Cook, skin side up, under a hot grill (broiler) until the skin blackens and blisters. Cool in a plastic bag, then peel the skin. Cut into thin strips.

3 Put the chicken between two sheets of plastic wrap and press with the palm of your hand until slightly flattened.

4 Heat 1 tablespoon of the oil in a large frying pan over medium heat. Add the chicken and cook for 2–3 minutes each side, or until cooked through. Remove from the pan and cut into 5 mm (¼ inch) slices.

5 Add 1 tablespoon of the oil to the pan and add the spring onion, sliced garlic and capsicum. Cook, stirring, for 2–3 minutes, or until starting to soften. Add 25 g (1 oz) of the mint, the vinegar and the remaining oil and stir.

6 Combine the pasta, chicken, spinach, spring onion mixture and remaining mint. Toss together and season.

LEMON-SCENTED BROTH WITH TORTELLINI

SERVES 4–6

1 lemon
125 ml (4 fl oz/½ cup) good quality white wine
440 g (14 oz) can chicken consomme
750 ml (27 fl oz/3 cups) water
30 g (1oz) chopped fresh parsley
black pepper, to taste
375 g (12 oz) fresh or dried veal- or chicken-filled tortellini
2 tablespoons freshly grated parmesan cheese, optional

1 Using a vegetable peeler, peel wide strips from lemon. Remove the white pith with a small sharp knife and cut 3 of the wide pieces into fine strips; set aside the fine strips for garnishing.

2 Place the wide lemon strips, white wine, consomme and water in a large deep pan. Cook for 10 minutes over low heat. Remove the lemon rind from the pan and bring mixture to the boil.

3 Add 2 tablespoons of parsley, pepper and tortellini to the pan. Cook for 6–7 minutes or until the pasta is just tender. Garnish with the remaining parsley and fine strips of lemon.

4 If desired, you can grate some parmesan to sprinkle over the top.

Note: If desired, the day before broth is required, follow the recipe to the removal of the lemon rind from the pan. Just before serving, bring the mixture to the boil; add the chopped parsley, black pepper and tortellini. Continue with the recipe. Variations: You can use chopped fresh basil instead of parsley. You can use different types of tortellini for this recipe.

BEAN SOUP WITH SAUSAGE

SERVES 4–6

4 Italian sausages

2 teaspoons olive oil

2 medium leeks, sliced

1 clove garlic, crushed

1 large carrot, chopped into small cubes

2 sticks celery, sliced

2 tablespoons plain flour

2 beef stock cubes, crumbled

2 litres (70 fl oz/8 cups) hot water

125 ml (4 fl oz/½ cup) white wine

125 g (4 oz) small shell pasta

440 g (14 oz) can three bean mix, drained

1 teaspoon chopped chilli (optional)

salt and pepper, to taste

1 Cut the sausages into small pieces.

2 Heat the oil in a large heavy-based pan and add the sausage pieces. Cook over a medium heat for 5 minutes or until golden, stirring regularly. Remove from the pan and drain on paper towels.

3 Add the leek, garlic, carrot and celery to the pan and cook for 2–3 minutes or until soft, stirring occasionally.

4 Add the flour, cook for 1 minute stirring constantly. Add the stock cubes, then gradually stir in the water and wine. Bring to the boil, reduce the heat and simmer, uncovered, for 10 minutes.

5 Add the pasta, beans and chilli to the pan. Increase the heat and cook for 8–10 minutes or until the pasta is tender. Return the sausage to the pan, add salt and pepper. Serve with chopped fresh parsley, if desired.

Note: Use dried beans, if preferred. Place in a bowl; cover with water; soak overnight. Drain; add to large pan with water to come about 3 cm above beans; simmer 1 hour. Drain well before adding to soup.

FUSILLI SALAD WITH SHERRY VINAIGRETTE

SERVES 6

300 g (10½ oz) fusilli

250 g (9 oz/2 cups) cauliflower

125 ml (4 fl oz/½ cup) olive oil

16 slices pancetta

1 small handful sage leaves

100 g (3½ oz/⅔ cup) pine nuts, toasted

2 tablespoons finely chopped red Asian shallots

1½ tablespoons sherry vinegar

1 small red chilli, finely chopped

2 garlic cloves, crushed

1 teaspoon soft brown sugar

2 tablespoons orange juice

1 handful flat-leaf (Italian) parsley, finely chopped

35 g (1¼ oz/⅓ cup) shaved parmesan cheese

1 Cook the pasta in a large saucepan of boiling salted water until al dente. Drain and refresh under cold water. Drain well. Blanch the cauliflower florets in boiling water for 3 minutes, then drain and allow to cool.

2 Heat 1 tablespoon of olive oil in a non-stick frying pan over medium heat and cook the pancetta for 2 minutes, or until crisp. Drain on paper towel.

3 Add 1 tablespoon of oil and cook the sage leaves for 1 minute, or until crisp. Drain on paper towel.

4 Combine the pasta, pine nuts and cauliflower in a bowl.

5 Heat the remaining olive oil, add the shallots and cook gently for 2 minutes, or until soft. Remove from the heat then add the vinegar, chilli, garlic, brown sugar, orange juice and chopped parsley.

6 Pour the warm dressing over the pasta and toss gently to combine.

7 Crumble the pancetta over the top and scatter with sage leaves and shaved parmesan. Serve warm.

PESTO BEEF SALAD

SERVES 4

100 g (4 oz) button mushrooms

1 large yellow capsicum (pepper)

1 large red capsicum (pepper)

cooking oil spray

100 g (4 oz) lean fillet steak

135 g (5 oz/1½ cups) penne

pesto (see recipe on page 8), or ready-
made

1 Cut the mushrooms into quarters. Cut the capsicums into large flat pieces, removing the seeds and membrane. Place skin-side-up under a hot grill until blackened. Leave covered with a tea towel (dish towel) until cool, then peel away the skin and chop the flesh.

2 Spray a non-stick frying pan with oil and cook the steak over high heat for 3–4 minutes each side until it is medium-rare. Remove and leave for 5 minutes before cutting into thin slices. Season with a little salt.

3 Meanwhile, cook the penne in a large pan of rapidly boiling salted water until just tender. Drain, then toss with the pesto in a large bowl.

4 Add the capsicum pieces, steak slices and mushroom quarters to the penne and toss to distribute evenly. Serve immediately.

MINESTRONE PRIMAVERA

SERVES 4–6

60 ml (2 fl oz/¼ cup) olive oil

45 g (1½ oz) pancetta, finely chopped

2 onions, chopped

2 garlic cloves, thinly sliced

2 small celery stalks, sliced

2 litres (70 fl oz/8 cups) chicken stock

50 g (1¾ oz/⅓ cup) macaroni

2 zucchini, chopped

150 g (5 oz/2 cups) shredded savoy cabbage

185 g (6 oz/1½ cups) green beans, chopped

155 g (5 oz/1 cup) frozen peas

40 g (1¼ oz/1 cup) shredded English spinach leaves

15 g (½ oz/¼ cup) chopped fresh basil

grated parmesan, for serving

1 **Put the oil,** pancetta, onion, garlic and celery in a large pan and stir occasionally over low heat for 8 minutes, or until the vegetables are soft but not brown.

2 **Add the stock** and bring to the boil. Simmer, covered, for 10 minutes.

3 **Add macaroni** and boil 12 minutes, or until almost tender.

4 **Stir in the zucchini,** cabbage, beans and peas and simmer for 5 minutes.

5 **Add the spinach** and basil and simmer for 2 minutes. Season to taste and serve with the grated Parmesan.

LAMB AND PASTA SOUP

SERVES 6–8

2 tablespoons oil

500 g (1 lb 2 oz) lean lamb meat, cut into bite-sized cubes

2 onions, finely chopped

2 carrots, chopped

4 celery stalks, chopped

425 g (14 oz) can crushed tomatoes

2 litres (70 fl oz/8 cups) beef stock

300 g (10 oz) spiral pasta

chopped fresh parsley, for serving

1 **Heat the oil** in a large pan and cook the lamb in batches until golden brown. Remove each batch as it is cooked and drain on paper towels.

2 **Add the onion** to the pan and cook for 2 minutes or until softened. Return all the meat to the pan.

3 **Add the carrot,** celery, tomato and beef stock. Stir to combine and bring to the boil. Reduce the heat to low and simmer, covered, for 15 minutes.

4 **Add the spiral pasta** to the soup. Stir briefly to prevent the pasta sticking to the pan. Simmer, uncovered, for another 15 minutes or until the lamb and pasta are tender.

5 **Sprinkle** with chopped parsley before serving.

Note: This soup can be kept, covered, in the fridge for up to 3 days. The pasta can be cooked separately, drained and added to the soup just before serving. For a lighter flavour, use half stock and half water. Vegetable stock can be used instead of beef.

PASTA-FILLED CAPSICUMS

SERVES 4–6

1 tablespoon olive oil

1 onion, finely chopped

1 clove garlic, crushed

3 rashers rindless bacon, finely chopped

150 g (5 oz) risoni, cooked

120 g (4 oz/1 cup) freshly grated
    mozzarella cheese

60 g (2 oz/½ cup) freshly grated
    parmesan cheese

2 tablespoons chopped fresh parsley

4 large red capsicum, halved lengthwise,
    seeds removed

425 g (14 oz) can tomatoes

125 ml (4 fl oz/½ cup) dry white wine

1 tablespoon tomato paste

½ teaspoon ground oregano

salt and freshly ground black pepper,
    to taste

2 tablespoons chopped fresh basil,
    to garnish

1 **Preheat the oven** to 180°C. Lightly oil a large shallow ovenproof dish.

2 **Heat the oil** in a pan. Add the onion and garlic and stir over a low heat until the onion is tender. Add the bacon and stir until crisp.

3 **Transfer the bacon mixture** to large bowl and combine with the risoni, cheeses and parsley. Spoon the mixture into the capsicum halves and arrange in the ovenproof dish.

4 **In a separate bowl,** combine the undrained, crushed tomatoes, wine, tomato paste, oregano, salt and pepper. Spoon the mixture into the capsicum halves. Sprinkle the chopped basil on top and Bake for 35–40 minutes.

VEGETARIAN

PENNE ALL'ARRABBIATA

SERVES 4

400 g (14 oz) penne

2 tablespoons olive oil

2 large garlic cloves, thinly sliced

1–2 dried chillies

800 g (1 lb 12 oz) tinned tomatoes

1 basil sprig, torn into pieces

1 Cook the pasta in a large saucepan of boiling salted water until just tender. Drain well and return to pan to keep warm.

2 Meanwhile, heat the olive oil in a saucepan over low heat. Add the garlic and chillies and cook until the garlic is light golden brown. Turn the chillies over during cooking so both sides get a chance to infuse in the oil.

3 Add the tomatoes and season with salt. Cook gently, breaking up the tomatoes with a wooden spoon, for 20–30 minutes, or until the sauce is rich and thick.

4 Add the basil to the sauce, toss with the pasta and season to taste.

ARTICHOKE RISONI

SERVES 4

30 g (1 oz) butter

1 tablespoon olive oil

2 fennel bulbs, sliced

340 g (12 oz) marinated artichoke hearts, drained and chopped

300 ml (10½ fl oz) pouring cream

1 tablespoon dijon mustard

3 tablespoons dry white wine

50 g (1¾ oz/½ cup) grated parmesan cheese

375 g (13 oz) risoni

130 g (4¾ oz) shredded English spinach

Italian bread, sliced, toasted, to serve

1 Heat the butter and oil in a frying pan over medium heat. Add the fennel and cook for 20 minutes, or until caramelised.

2 Add the artichoke and cook for a further 5–10 minutes.

3 Stir in the cream, mustard, white wine and parmesan and bring to the boil. Reduce the heat and simmer for 5 minutes.

4 Meanwhile, cook the pasta in a large saucepan of boiling salted water until just tender. Drain well and return to the pan to keep warm.

5 Add the pasta and spinach to the sauce and cook until the spinach has wilted. Serve with toasted Italian bread.

ORECCHIETTE WITH BABY SPINACH AND PUMPKIN

SERVES 4

750 g (1 lb 10 oz) pumpkin (winter squash), such as butternut or jap

2 tablespoons parmesan-infused olive oil (see Note)

16 unpeeled garlic cloves

250 g (9 oz) cherry tomatoes, halved

500 g (1 lb 2 oz) orecchiette

200 g (7 oz) baby English spinach leaves

200 g (7 oz) marinated Persian feta cheese (see Note)

3 tablespoons sherry vinegar

2 tablespoons walnut oil

1   **Preheat the oven** to 200°C (400°F/Gas 6). Cut the pumpkin into large cubes, put in a roasting tin and drizzle with the parmesan-infused oil. Roast for 30 minutes, then add the garlic.

2   **Arrange the tomatoes** on a baking tray. Place all the vegetables in the oven and roast for 10–15 minutes, or until cooked. Don't overcook the tomatoes.

3   **Meanwhile,** cook the pasta in a large saucepan of boiling salted water until just tender. Drain well and return to the pan to keep warm.

4   **Toss together the pasta,** tomatoes, pumpkin, garlic and spinach in a large bowl.

5   **Drain the feta,** reserving 3 tablespoons of marinade. Whisk the reserved marinade, sherry vinegar and walnut oil together. Pour over the pasta and sprinkle with pieces of the feta.

Note: Parmesan-infused olive oil is available at gourmet food stores and adds depth of flavour. Persian feta is softer and creamier than other types of feta. It is marinated in oil, herbs and garlic.

SEMOLINA GNOCCHI

SERVES 4

3 spring onions, chopped

200 g (7 oz) baby mushrooms, sliced

2 tablespoons plain flour

375 ml (12 fl oz/1½ cups) milk

125 ml (4 fl oz/½ cup) thick (double/heavy) cream

125 g (4 oz) freshly grated gruyère cheese (see Note)

salt and pepper, to taste

80 g (3oz/½ cup) pine nuts, toasted

1 Bring a large pan of water to the boil. Add the tortellini and cook until just tender. Drain and keep warm.

2 Melt half the butter in a medium pan, add the spring onion and sliced mushrooms. Cook over a medium heat for 3 minutes or until softened. Set aside.

3 In another pan, melt the remaining butter. Add the flour and stir over low heat for 2 minutes. Gradually add the milk and cream, stirring constantly until the sauce boils and thickens.

4 Add the cheese and season to taste, stir well. Combine the sauce with the mushrooms.

5 To serve, arrange the tortellini in a serving bowl, pour the sauce over and sprinkle with pine nuts and extra chopped spring onion, if desired.

Note: Gruyère is a hard full-flavoured cheese that melts easily.

BEETROOT RAVIOLI WITH SAGE BURNT BUTTER SAUCE

SERVES 4

340 g (12 oz) tinned baby beetroot (beets)

40 g (1½ oz/⅓ cup) grated parmesan cheese

250 g (9 oz/1 cup) fresh ricotta cheese

4 fresh lasagne sheets

fine cornmeal, for sprinkling

200 g (7 oz) butter, chopped

1 tablespoon sage leaves, torn

2 garlic cloves, crushed

shaved parmesan cheese, to serve

1 **Drain the beetroot,** then grate it into a bowl. Add the parmesan and ricotta and mix well.

2 **Lay a sheet of pasta** on a flat surface and place evenly spaced tablespoons of the ricotta mixture on the pasta to give 12 mounds — four across and three down. Flatten the mounds of filling slightly. Lightly brush the edges of the pasta sheet and around each pile of filling with water.

3 **Place a second sheet of pasta** over the top and press around each mound to seal and enclose the filling. Using a pasta wheel or sharp knife, cut the pasta into 12 ravioli.

4 **Lay them out** on a lined baking tray that has been sprinkled with cornmeal. Repeat with the remaining filling and lasagne sheets to make 24 ravioli. Gently remove any air bubbles after cutting so that they are completely sealed.

5 **Cook the pasta** in a large saucepan of boiling salted water until just tender. Drain well, then divide among four serving plates.

6 **Meanwhile,** melt the butter in a saucepan until golden brown. Remove from the heat, stir in the sage and garlic and spoon over the ravioli. Sprinkle with shaved parmesan and season before serving.

ROASTED VEGETABLE CANNELLONI

SERVES 4

60 g (2 oz) butter
1 large leek, cut into 1 cm (½ inch) pieces
200 g (7 oz) chargrilled eggplant (aubergine) in oil
200 g (7 oz) chargrilled orange sweet potato in oil
125 g (4½ oz/1 cup) grated cheddar cheese
40 g (1½ oz/⅓ cup) plain (all-purpose) flour
1 litre (35 fl oz/4 cups) milk
6 fresh lasagne sheets

1 **Preheat the oven** to 200°C (400°F/Gas 6). Lightly grease a 28 x 18 x 5 cm (11¼ x 7 x 2 inch) ceramic dish. Melt 20 g (¾ oz) of the butter in a saucepan, add the leek and stir over medium heat for 8 minutes, or until soft.

2 **Chop the eggplant** and sweet potato into 1 cm (½ inch) pieces and place in a bowl. Mix in the leek and 40 g (1½ oz/ ¼ cup) of the cheddar.

3 **Melt the remaining butter** in a saucepan over medium heat. Stir in the flour and cook for 1 minute, or until foaming. Remove from the heat and gradually stir in the milk. Return to the heat and stir until the sauce boils and thickens. Reduce the heat and simmer for 2 minutes. Season.

4 **Stir 375 ml** (13 fl oz/1½ cups) of the sauce into the vegetable mixture, adding extra if necessary to bind it together.

5 **Cut the lasagne sheets** in half widthways to make two smaller rectangles. Spoon the vegetable mixture along the centre of one sheet and roll up. Repeat to make 12 tubes in total.

6 **Place the tubes,** seam side down, in the dish and spoon the remaining sauce over the top until they are covered. Sprinkle with the remaining cheese and bake for about 20 minutes, or until the top is golden.

CASARECCE WITH GOAT'S CHEESE

SERVES 4

16 roma (plum) tomatoes

1 handful basil leaves, torn

400 g (14 oz) casarecce

4 tablespoons olive oil

2 garlic cloves, finely sliced

2 tablespoons lemon juice

120 g (4¼ oz) rocket (arugula),
roughly chopped

2 tablespoons chopped flat-leaf
(Italian) parsley

35 g (1¼ oz/⅓ cup) grated
parmesan cheese

100 g (3½ oz) goat's cheese, crumbled

1 **Preheat the oven** to 160°C (315°F/Gas 2–3).

2 **Score a cross** in the base of the tomatoes. Put in a heatproof bowl, and cover with boiling water. Leave for about 30 seconds, then transfer to cold water and peel the skin away from the cross. Cut in half and place cut-side up on a wire rack over a baking tray. Season liberally and scatter with the basil leaves. Put the tray in the oven and bake for 3 hours.

3 **Meanwhile,** cook the pasta in a large saucepan of boiling salted water until just tender. Drain well and return to the pan to keep warm.

4 **Heat the olive oil** and garlic over low–medium heat until it just begins to sizzle. Remove immediately and add to the pasta with the tomatoes, lemon juice, rocket, parsley and parmesan. Stir gently to combine, allowing the heat from the pasta to wilt the rocket.

5 **Serve** topped with the crumbled goat's cheese.

ORECCHIETTE WITH BROCCOLI

SERVES 6

750 g (1 lb 10 oz) broccoli, cut into florets
450 g (1 lb) orecchiette
3 tablespoons extra virgin olive oil
½ teaspoon dried chilli flakes
30 g (1 oz/⅓ cup) grated pecorino or parmesan cheese

1   Blanch the broccoli in a large saucepan of boiling salted water for 5 minutes, or until just tender. Remove with a slotted spoon, drain well and return the water to the boil.

2   Cook the pasta in the boiling water until al dente. Drain well and return to the pan to keep warm.

3   Meanwhile, heat the oil in a heavy-based frying pan over medium heat. Add the chilli flakes and broccoli and cook, stirring, for 5 minutes, or until the broccoli is well coated and beginning to break apart. Season.

4   Add to the pasta, stir through the cheese and serve.

EGGPLANT, RICOTTA AND PASTA POTS

SERVES 4

200 g (7 oz) straight macaroni

125 ml (4 fl oz/½ cup) light olive oil

1 large eggplant (aubergine), cut lengthways into 1 cm (½ inch) slices

1 small onion, finely chopped

2 garlic cloves, crushed

420 g (14 oz) tinned chopped tomatoes

400 g (13 oz) ricotta cheese

80 g (2¾ oz/1 cup) coarsely grated parmesan cheese

15 g (½ oz/¼ cup) shredded basil, plus extra to garnish

1 **Preheat the oven** to 180°C (350°F/Gas 4). Cook the pasta in a large saucepan of boiling salted water until just tender. Drain well and return to the pan to keep warm.

2 **Heat 2 tablespoons** of the oil in a non-stick frying pan over medium heat. Cook the eggplant in three batches for 2–3 minutes on each side, or until golden, adding 2 tablespoons of oil with each batch. Remove and drain well on paper towels.

3 **Add the onion** and garlic to the pan and cook over medium heat for 2–3 minutes, or until just golden.

4 **Add the tomato** and cook for 5 minutes, or until most of the liquid has evaporated. Season.

5 **Combine the ricotta,** parmesan, basil and pasta in a bowl.

6 **Line the base and sides** of four 375 ml (13 fl oz/1½ cup) ramekins with eggplant, trimming any overhanging pieces. Top with half the pasta mix, pressing down firmly. Spoon over the tomato sauce, then cover with the remaining pasta mixture.

7 **Bake for 10–15 minutes,** or until heated through. Stand for 5 minutes, then run a knife around the ramekin to loosen. Invert onto plates and garnish with basil.

CASARECCE WITH PUMPKIN AND FETA

SERVES 4

1 kg (2 lb 4 oz) butternut pumpkin
(squash), peeled and cut into 2 cm
(¾ inch) chunks

1 red onion, thinly sliced

8 garlic cloves, unpeeled

1 tablespoon rosemary leaves

4 tablespoons olive oil

400 g (14 oz) casarecce

200 g (7 oz) marinated feta cheese,
crumbled

2 tablespoons grated parmesan cheese

2 tablespoons finely chopped flat-leaf
(Italian) parsley

1 **Preheat the oven** to 200°C (400°F/Gas 6). Place pumpkin, onion, garlic and rosemary in a roasting tin. Drizzle with 1 tablespoon of the oil and season. Rub the oil over all the vegetables and herbs until well coated. Roast for 30 minutes, or until the pumpkin is soft and starting to caramelize.

2 **Cook the pasta** in a large saucepan of boiling salted water until just tender. Drain well and return to pan to keep warm.

3 **Squeeze the roasted garlic** out of its skin and place it in a bowl with the remaining oil. Mash with a fork.

4 **Add the garlic oil** to the pasta, then stir through the remaining ingredients. Toss to combine. Season to taste.

ZUCCHINI PASTA BAKE

SERVES 4

200 g (7 oz) risoni

40 g (1½ oz) butter

4 spring onions (scallions), thinly sliced

400 g (14 oz) zucchini (courgettes), grated

4 eggs

125 ml (4 fl oz/½ cup) pouring cream

120 g (4 oz) ricotta cheese (see Note)

100 g (3½ oz/⅔ cup) grated mozzarella cheese

75 g (2½ oz/¾ cup) grated parmesan cheese

1 **Preheat the oven** to 180°C (350°F/Gas 4).

2 **Cook the pasta** in a large saucepan of boiling salted water until just tender. Drain well and return to pan to keep warm.

3 **Meanwhile,** heat the butter in a frying pan over medium heat. Add the spring onion and cook for 1 minute. Add the zucchini and cook for a further 4 minutes, or until soft. Allow to cool slightly.

4 **Combine the eggs,** cream, ricotta, mozzarella, pasta and half of the parmesan. Stir in the zucchini mixture. Season well.

5 **Spoon into four 500 ml** (17 fl oz/2 cup) greased ovenproof dishes. Sprinkle with the remaining parmesan and bake for 25–30 minutes, or until firm and golden.

Note: With such simple flavours, it is important to use good-quality fresh ricotta from the delicatessen or the deli section of your local supermarket.

PENNE WITH TOMATO AND BASIL SAUCE

SERVES 4

500 g (1 lb 2 oz) penne rigate

4 tablespoons extra virgin olive oil

4 garlic cloves, crushed

4 anchovy fillets, finely chopped

2 small red chillies, seeded and finely chopped

6 large vine-ripened tomatoes, peeled, seeded and diced

4 tablespoons white wine

1 tablespoon tomato paste (concentrated purée)

2 teaspoons sugar

2 tablespoons finely chopped flat-leaf (Italian) parsley

3 tablespoons shredded basil

grated parmesan cheese, to serve (optional)

1 Cook the pasta in a large saucepan of boiling salted water until just tender. Drain well and return to pan to keep warm.

2 Meanwhile, heat the oil in a frying pan over medium heat. Cook the garlic for 30 seconds. Stir in the anchovy and chilli and cook for a further 30 seconds.

3 Increase the heat to high, add the tomato and cook for 2 minutes.

4 Add the wine, tomato paste and sugar and simmer, covered, for 10 minutes, or until thickened.

5 Toss the tomato sauce and herbs through the pasta. Season and serve with grated parmesan, if desired.

CONCHIGLIE RIGATE WITH SPRING VEGETABLES

SERVES 4

500 g (1 lb 2 oz) conchiglie rigate

310 g (11 oz/2 cups) frozen peas

310 g (11 oz/2 cups) frozen broad (fava) beans, blanched and peeled

4 tablespoons olive oil

6 spring onions (scallions), cut into 3 cm (1¼ inch) pieces

2 garlic cloves, finely chopped

250 ml (9 fl oz/1 cup) vegetable or chicken stock

12 thin fresh asparagus spears, cut into 5 cm (2 inch) lengths

½ teaspoon finely grated lemon zest

3 tablespoons lemon juice

shaved parmesan cheese, to garnish

1 **Cook the pasta** in a large saucepan of boiling salted water until just tender. Drain well and return to pan to keep warm.

2 **Meanwhile,** put the peas in a saucepan of boiling water and cook over high heat for 1–2 minutes, or until tender. Remove with a slotted spoon and plunge into cold water.

3 **Add the broad beans** to the saucepan of boiling water and cook for 1–2 minutes, then drain and plunge into cold water. Remove and slip the skins off.

4 **Heat 2 tablespoons** of the oil in a frying pan over medium heat. Add the spring onion and garlic and cook for 2 minutes, or until softened.

5 **Pour in the stock** and cook for 5 minutes, or until slightly reduced. Add the asparagus and cook for 3–4 minutes, or until bright green and just tender.

6 **Stir in the peas** and broad beans and cook for about 3 minutes, or until heated through.

7 **Toss the remaining oil** through the pasta, then add the vegetables, lemon zest and lemon juice. Season and toss together well. Serve topped with shaved parmesan.

PORCINI MUSHROOM AND WALNUT PENNE

SERVES 4

20 g (¾ oz) porcini mushrooms

400 g (14 oz) penne rigate

2 tablespoons olive oil

1 onion, finely chopped

2 garlic cloves, crushed

24 button mushrooms, sliced

3 thyme sprigs

90 g (3¼ oz/¾ cup) walnuts

2 tablespoons sour cream

grated parmesan cheese, to serve

1 Put the porcini in a bowl with just enough boiling water to cover and leave to soak for 30 minutes. If they soak up all the water quickly, add a little more.

2 Cook the pasta in a large saucepan of boiling salted water until just tender. Drain well and return to pan to keep warm.

3 Heat the oil in a deep frying pan over medium heat. Add the onion and garlic and cook until translucent but not browned. Add the porcini and any soaking liquid, mushrooms and thyme. The mushrooms will give off liquid as they cook so continue cooking until the liquid is soaked up again.

4 In a separate frying pan, fry the walnuts over medium heat without any oil until they start to brown and smell toasted. Allow to cool slightly, then roughly chop and add to the mushroom mixture.

5 Toss with the pasta, stir through the sour cream and season. Serve with the parmesan.

PENNE WITH TOMATO AND ONION JAM AND OLIVES

SERVES 4

3 tablespoons olive oil

4 red onions, sliced

1 tablespoon soft brown sugar

2 tablespoons balsamic vinegar

800 g (1 lb 12 oz) tinned chopped
    tomatoes

500 g (1 lb 2 oz) penne rigate

150 g (5½ oz/scant 1 cup) small pitted
    black olives

75 g (2½ oz/¾ cup) grated parmesan
    cheese

1 Heat the oil in a non-stick frying pan over medium heat. Add the onion and sugar and cook for 25–30 minutes, or until caramelised.

2 Stir in the vinegar, bring to the boil and cook for 5 minutes.

3 Add the tomatoes, return to the boil, then reduce the heat to medium–low and simmer for about 25 minutes, or until the tomatoes are reduced and jam-like.

4 Meanwhile, cook the pasta in a large saucepan of boiling salted water until just tender. Drain well and return to the pan to keep warm.

5 Add the tomato mixture and olives and stir to combine. Season and top with the grated parmesan.

PUMPKIN, SPINACH AND RICOTTA LASAGNE

SERVES 4

3 tablespoons olive oil

1.5 kg (3 lb 5 oz) butternut pumpkin
    (squash), cut into 1.5 cm (⅝ inch) dice

500 g (1 lb 2 oz) English spinach leaves

4 fresh lasagne sheets

500 g (1 lb 2 oz/2 cups) ricotta cheese

2 tablespoons pouring cream

25 g (1 oz/¼ cup) grated parmesan
    cheese

pinch ground nutmeg

1 Heat the oil in a non-stick frying pan over medium heat. Add the pumpkin and cook, stirring occasionally, for 15 minutes, or until tender. Season and keep warm.

2 Cook the spinach in a large saucepan of boiling water for 30 seconds, or until wilted. Using a slotted spoon, transfer to a bowl of cold water. Drain well and squeeze out as much excess water as possible. Finely chop the spinach.

3 Add the lasagne sheets to the saucepan of boiling water and cook, stirring occasionally, until al dente. Drain. Cut each sheet widthways into thirds.

4 Combine the ricotta, cream, parmesan, spinach and nutmeg in a small saucepan over low heat. Stir for about 3 minutes, or until warmed through.

5 Place a piece of lasagne on the base of each plate. Spoon half the pumpkin onto each of the sheets, then cover with another piece of lasagne. Use half the ricotta mixture to spread over the lasagne sheets, then add another lasagne piece. Top with the remaining pumpkin, then remaining ricotta mixture. Season well and serve immediately.

CONCHIGLIONE WITH ROAST PUMPKIN AND RICOTTA

SERVES 6

1 kg (2 lb 4 oz) butternut pumpkin (squash), cut into large wedges

olive oil, to drizzle

10 unpeeled garlic cloves

500 g (1 lb 2 oz) ricotta cheese

1 handful finely shredded basil

750 ml (26 fl oz/3 cups) ready-made tomato pasta sauce

125 ml (4 fl oz/½ cup) dry white wine

56 conchiglione or 32 giant conchiglione

100 g (3½ oz/1 cup) grated parmesan cheese

1   Preheat the oven to 200°C (400°F/Gas 6). Place the pumpkin in a baking dish, drizzle with olive oil and season. Bake for 30 minutes, then add the garlic and bake for 15 minutes or until tender. Allow to cool slightly, then peel and mash the pumpkin and garlic.

2   Mix with the ricotta and half the basil and season to taste.

3   Put the pasta sauce and wine in a saucepan and bring to the boil over medium heat. Reduce the heat and simmer for 10 minutes, or until slightly thickened.

4   Meanwhile, cook the pasta in a large saucepan of boiling salted water until just tender. Drain well. Lay out on a tea towel (dish towel) to dry, then fill with the pumpkin mixture. Spread any remaining filling in a large ovenproof dish, top with the shells and pour on the sauce.

5   Sprinkle with parmesan and the remaining basil and bake for about 15–20 minutes (or 30 minutes for the giant shells).

SPINACH AND RICOTTA RAVIOLI

1 tablespoon olive oil
1 red onion, finely chopped
1 garlic clove, crushed
200 g (7 oz/5 cups) baby English spinach leaves, coarsely chopped
250 g (9 oz/1 cup) ricotta cheese
2 egg yolks, beaten
2 tablespoons grated parmesan cheese
freshly grated nutmeg
48 won ton wrappers
40 g (1½ oz) butter
2 tablespoons sage leaves

1 Heat the oil in a frying pan over low heat. Add the onion and garlic and fry for 2–3 minutes, or until the onion is soft and translucent. Add the spinach and stir until wilted.

2 Stir the spinach mixture into the ricotta, along with the egg yolk, parmesan and some nutmeg. Season.

3 Brush a little water around the edge of a won ton wrapper and put 1 teaspoon of filling in the centre. Fold the wrapper over to make a half moon shape and press the edges firmly together. Lay out the ravioli on a tea towel (dish towel) and repeat with the remaining wrappers.

4 Cook the pasta in a large saucepan of boiling salted water until just tender. Remove with a slotted spoon and drain well.

5 Melt the butter in a small saucepan over medium heat. Add the sage and cook for 1–2 minutes, or until the butter browns slightly. Pour the butter and sage mixture over the pasta and serve.

PASTA ALLA NORMA

SERVES 4–6

185 ml (6 fl oz/¾ cup) olive oil

1 onion, finely chopped

2 garlic cloves, finely chopped

800 g (1 lb 12 oz) tinned chopped
    tomatoes

400 g (14 oz) bucatini

1 large eggplant (aubergine), about
    500 g (1 lb 2 oz)

1 very large handful basil leaves, torn,
    plus extra, to garnish

60 g (2¼ oz/½ cup) ricotta salata,
    crumbled (see Note)

45 g (1½ oz/½ cup) grated pecorino or
    parmesan cheese

1 tablespoon extra virgin olive oil, to
    drizzle

1 Heat **2 tablespoons** of the oil in a frying pan over medium heat. Cook the onion for 5 minutes. Stir in the garlic and cook for 30 seconds. Add the tomato and season. Reduce the heat to low and cook for 20–25 minutes, or until thick.

2 **Cook the pasta** in a large saucepan of boiling salted water until just tender. Drain well and return to pan to keep warm.

3 **Meanwhile,** cut the eggplant lengthways into 5 mm (¼ inch) thick slices. Heat the remaining olive oil in a large frying pan over medium heat. Add the eggplant slices a few at a time and cook for 3–5 minutes, or until lightly browned on both sides. Remove from the pan and drain on crumpled paper towel.

4 **Add the eggplant** to the sauce with the basil, stirring over very low heat. Add the pasta to the sauce with half each of the ricotta and pecorino and toss together.

5 **Serve** sprinkled with the remaining cheeses and basil and drizzle with oil.

Note: Ricotta salata is a lightly salted, pressed ricotta cheese. If unavailable, use a mild feta cheese.

FETTUCINE WITH CREAMY SPINACH AND ROAST TOMATO

SERVES 4–6

6 roma (plum) tomatoes

2 tablespoons butter

2 garlic cloves, crushed

1 onion, chopped

500 g (1 lb 2 oz) English spinach

250 ml (8 fl oz/1 cup) vegetable stock

125 ml (4 fl oz/½ cup) thick (double/ heavy) cream

500 g (1 lb) fresh spinach fettucine

60 g (2 oz/½ cup) shaved parmesan

1 **Preheat the oven** to 220°C (425°F/Gas 7). Cut the tomatoes in half lengthways, then cut each half into three wedges. Place the wedges on a lightly greased baking tray and roast for 30–35 minutes, or until softened and slightly golden.

2 **Meanwhile,** heat the butter in a large frying pan over medium heat. Add the garlic and onion and cook for 5 minutes, or until the onion is soft.

3 **Add the spinach,** stock and cream. Increase the heat to high and bring to the boil. Simmer for 5 minutes. Remove from the heat and season. Set aside to cool slightly.

4 **Meanwhile,** cook the pasta in a large saucepan of boiling salted water until al dente. Drain well and return to the pan to keep warm.

5 **Process the spinach** mixture in a food processor until smooth. Toss through the pasta until well coated. Top with the roasted tomatoes and parmesan.

ROASTED CHUNKY RATATOUILLE CANNELLONI

SERVES 6–8

1 eggplant (aubergine)

2 zucchini (courgettes)

1 large red capsicum (pepper)

1 large green capsicum (pepper)

3–4 ripe roma (plum) tomatoes

12 unpeeled garlic cloves

3 tablespoons olive oil

300 ml (10½ fl oz/1¼ cups) tomato passata (puréed tomatoes)

350 g (12 oz/⅔ cup) cannelloni tubes

3 tablespoons shredded basil

300 g (10½ oz/⅓ cup) ricotta cheese

100 g (3½ oz) feta cheese

1 egg, lightly beaten

50 g (1¾ oz) pecorino pepato cheese, grated

1 Preheat the oven to 200°C (400°F/Gas 6). Cut the eggplant, zucchini, capsicums and tomatoes into 2 cm (¾ inch) cubes and place in a baking dish with the garlic. Drizzle with the oil and toss to coat. Bake for 1 hour 30 minutes, or until the vegetables are tender and the tomatoes slightly mushy. Peel and lightly mash the garlic cloves.

2 Pour the passata over the base of a large ovenproof dish. Spoon the ratatouille into the cannelloni tubes and arrange in the dish.

3 Combine the basil, ricotta, feta and egg in a bowl. Season well and spoon over the cannelloni. Sprinkle with the pecorino and bake for 30 minutes, or until the cannelloni is soft.

SWEET POTATO RAVIOLI

SERVES 4

500 g (1 lb 2 oz) orange sweet potato, chopped

2 teaspoons lemon juice

190 g (6¾ oz) butter

50 g (1¾ oz/½ cup) grated parmesan cheese

1 tablespoon snipped chives

1 egg, lightly beaten

250 g (9 oz) packet won ton wrappers

2 tablespoons sage, torn

2 tablespoons chopped walnuts

1 **Cook the sweet potato** and lemon juice in a large saucepan of boiling water for 15 minutes, or until tender. Drain and pat dry with paper towel. Allow to cool for 5 minutes.

2 **Blend the sweet potato** and 30 g (1 oz) of the butter in a food processor until smooth. Add the parmesan, chives and half the egg. Season and set aside to cool.

3 **Brush a little** of the egg mixture around the edges of half the won ton wrappers. Put 2 teaspoons of the mixture in the centre of half the won ton wrappers. Cover with the remaining wrappers and press the edges firmly together. Using a 7 cm (2¾ inch) cutter, cut the ravioli into circles.

4 **Melt the remaining butter** in a small saucepan over low heat and cook until golden brown.

5 **Meanwhile,** cook the pasta in a large saucepan of boiling salted water until just tender. Remove with a slotted spoon and drain well.

6 **Serve** immediately, drizzled with the butter and sprinkled with the sage and walnuts.

SPAGHETTINI WITH ASPARAGUS AND ROCKET

SERVES 4

100 ml (3½ fl oz) extra virgin olive oil

16 thin asparagus spears, cut into 5 cm (2 inch) lengths

375 g (13 oz) spaghettini

120 g (4¼ oz) rocket (arugula), shredded

2 small red chillies, finely chopped

2 teaspoons finely grated lemon zest

1 garlic clove, finely chopped

100 g (3½ oz/1 cup) grated parmesan cheese

2 tablespoons lemon juice

1 **Bring a large saucepan** of water to the boil over medium heat. Add 1 tablespoon of the oil and a pinch of salt to the water and blanch the asparagus for 3–4 minutes. Remove the asparagus with a slotted spoon, refresh under cold water, drain and place in a bowl.

2 **Return the water** to a rapid boil and add the spaghettini. Cook the pasta until just tender. Drain well and return to the pan to keep warm.

3 **Meanwhile,** add the rocket, chilli, lemon zest, garlic and 65 g (2¼ oz/⅔ cup) of parmesan to the asparagus. Mix well.

4 **Add to the pasta,** pour on the lemon juice and remaining olive oil and season. Stir well to combine. Top with the remaining parmesan.

BUCKWHEAT PASTA WITH CHEESE SAUCE

SERVES 6

350 g (12 oz) savoy cabbage, roughly chopped
175 g (6 oz) potatoes, cut into 2 cm (¾ inch) cubes
500 g (1 lb 2 oz) buckwheat pasta (see Note)
4 tablespoons extra virgin olive oil
30 g (1 oz) sage, finely chopped
2 garlic cloves, finely chopped
350 g (12 oz) mixed cheeses (such as mascarpone, fontina, taleggio and gorgonzola)
grated parmesan cheese, to serve

1 Bring a large saucepan of salted water to the boil. Add the cabbage, potato and the pasta and cook for 3–5 minutes, or until the pasta is just tender and the vegetables are cooked. Drain well, reserving about 250 ml (9 fl oz/1 cup) of the cooking water.

2 Add the olive oil to the saucepan and gently cook the sage and garlic for about 1 minute.

3 Add the mixed cheeses to the pan. Stir, then add the pasta, cabbage and potatoes. Season.

4 Remove the saucepan from the heat and gently stir the mixture together, adding some of the reserved pasta water to loosen it up a little if necessary. Serve with parmesan.

Note: Buckwheat pasta is called pizzoccheri in Italy. This type of pasta is popular in Valtellina, near the Swiss border, and is traditionally served with potatoes, cabbage and cheese.

FUSILLI WITH ROASTED TOMATOES AND BOCCONCINI

SERVES 4–6

800 g (1 lb 12 oz) cherry or teardrop tomatoes (or a mixture of both), halved if they are large

500 g (1 lb 2 oz) fusilli

300 g (10½ oz) baby bocconcini (fresh baby mozzarella cheese), sliced

1 tablespoon chopped thyme

TAPENADE

1½ tablespoons capers

2 small garlic cloves

185 g (6½ oz/1½ cups) sliced black olives

3 tablespoons lemon juice

4–5 tablespoons extra virgin olive oil

1 **Preheat the oven** to 200°C (400°F/Gas 6). Place the tomatoes on a baking tray, season and roast for 10 minutes, or until slightly dried.

2 **To make the tapenade,** put the capers, garlic, olives and lemon juice in a food processor and mix together. With the motor running, gradually add the oil until the mixture forms a smooth paste.

3 **Cook the pasta** in a large saucepan of boiling salted water until al dente. Drain well and return to the pan to keep warm.

4 **Toss the tapenade** and bocconcini through the pasta. Top with the tomatoes and thyme.

ORZO AND GREEK CHEESE BAKE

SERVES 4–6

415 g (14¾ oz/2 cups) orzo (rice-shaped pasta)
60 g (2¼ oz) butter
6 spring onions (scallions), chopped
450 g (1 lb/10 cups) English spinach, stems removed, rinsed well and chopped
2 tablespoons plain (all-purpose) flour
1.25 litres (44 fl oz/5 cups) milk
250 g (9 oz 1 ⅔ cups) kefalotyri cheese, grated (see Note)
250 g (9 oz/1 ⅔ cups) marinated feta cheese, well drained
3 tablespoons chopped dill

1 **Preheat the oven** to 190°C (375°F/Gas 5).

2 **Cook the pasta** in a large saucepan of boiling salted water until just tender. Drain well, then return to the pan.

3 **Heat 20 g** (¾ oz) of the butter in a large saucepan over high heat and cook the spring onion for 30 seconds.

4 **Add the spinach** and stir for 1 minute. Season and stir into the orzo.

5 **Put the remaining butter** in the pan in which the spinach was cooked. Melt over low heat, then stir in the flour and cook for 1 minute, or until pale and foaming. Remove from the heat and gradually stir in the milk. Return to the heat and stir constantly for 5 minutes, or until the sauce boils and thickens.

6 **Add two-thirds** of the kefalotyri and all of the feta and stir for 2 minutes, or until melted and well mixed. Remove from the heat and stir in the dill.

7 **Combine the pasta mixture** with the cheese sauce, season and pour into a greased 2.5 litre (88 fl oz/10 cup) ovenproof ceramic dish. Sprinkle the remaining cheese over the top and bake for 15 minutes, or until golden.

Note: Kefalotyri is a hard Greek sheep's or goat's milk cheese. parmesan or pecorino cheese can be substituted.

FRESH VEGETABLE LASAGNE WITH ROCKET

SERVES 4

BALSAMIC SYRUP

4 tablespoons balsamic vinegar

1½ tablespoons brown sugar

16 asparagus spears, trimmed and cut into 5 cm (2 inch) lengths

150 g (5½ oz/1 cup) peas

2 large zucchini (courgettes), cut into thin ribbons

2 fresh lasagne sheets

100 g (3½ oz) rocket (arugula)

1 large handful basil, torn

2 tablespoons olive oil

250 g (9 oz/1 cup) ricotta cheese

150 g (5½ oz) semi-dried (sun-blushed) tomatoes

shaved parmesan cheese, to serve

1 **To make the balsamic syrup,** stir the vinegar and brown sugar in a saucepan over medium heat until the sugar dissolves. Reduce the heat and simmer for 3–4 minutes. Remove from the heat.

2 **Bring a saucepan** of salted water to the boil. Blanch the asparagus, peas and zucchini in separate batches until just tender. Remove and refresh each batch in cold water and drain well.

3 **Return the cooking liquid** to the boil. Cook the lasagne sheets in the water for 1–2 minutes, or until just tender. Drain. Cut each sheet in half lengthways..

4 **Toss the vegetables** and the rocket with the basil and olive oil. Season.

5 **Place one strip** of pasta on a plate — one-third on the centre of the plate and two-thirds overhanging one side. Place some salad on the centre one-third, topped with some ricotta and tomato. Season and fold over one-third of the lasagne sheet. Top with another layer of salad, ricotta and tomato. Fold back the final layer of pasta and garnish with salad and tomato. Repeat with the remaining pasta, salad, ricotta and tomato.

6 **Drizzle with the balsamic syrup** and serve with the parmesan.

ROAST PUMPKIN SAUCE ON PAPPARDELLE

SERVES 4

1.5 kg (3 lb) butternut pumpkin, cut into small cubes

4 garlic cloves, crushed

3 teaspoons fresh thyme leaves

100 ml (3½ fl oz) olive oil

500 g (1 lb) pappardelle

2 tablespoons cream

185 ml (6 fl oz/¾ cup) hot vegetable stock

30 g (1 oz/¼ cup) shaved parmesan, to serve

extra thyme leaves, to serve

1 **Preheat the oven** to 200°C (400°F/Gas 6).

2 **Combine the pumpkin,** garlic, thyme and 3 tablespoons of the olive oil in a bowl and toss together. Season.

3 **Transfer to a baking tray** and cook for 30 minutes, or until tender and golden.

4 **Meanwhile,** cook the pasta in a large saucepan of boiling salted water until just tender. Drain well and return to the pan to keep warm. Toss through the remaining oil and keep warm.

5 **Place the pumpkin** and the cream in a food processor or blender and process until smooth. Add the hot stock and process until smooth and combined. Season and gently toss through the pasta.

6 **Serve** sprinkled with parmesan and extra thyme, if desired.

FREEFORM RICOTTA AND MUSHROOM LASAGNE

SERVES 4

250 g (9 oz/1 cup) ricotta cheese

65 g (2¼ oz/⅔cup) grated parmesan cheese

3½ tablespoons olive oil

1 onion, thinly sliced

2 garlic cloves, crushed

500 g (1 lb 2 oz) swiss brown mushrooms, sliced

300 ml (10½ fl oz) ready-made tomato pasta sauce

6 sheets fresh lasagne, cut in half, then cut into 12 cm (4½ inch) squares

200 g (7 oz/8 cups) baby English spinach leaves, washed

1 Mix the ricotta with half the parmesan and season.

2 Heat 2 tablespoons of oil in a large frying pan, add the onion and cook for 2 minutes, or until it softens.

3 Add the garlic and mushrooms and cook for 1–2 minutes, or until the mushrooms start to soften.

4 Add the tomato pasta sauce and cook for a further 5–6 minutes, or until the sauce starts to thicken. Season well.

5 Meanwhile, cook the pasta in a large saucepan of boiling salted water until just tender. Drain well and return to the pan to keep warm.

6 Put the spinach in a pan with just the water clinging to the leaves. Cover and cook over medium heat for 1–2 minutes, or until the spinach has wilted.

7 To assemble, place a pasta square on the base of each plate. Top with the mushroom sauce, then place another pasta square on top. Spread the ricotta mixture evenly over the surface, leaving a 2 cm (¾ inch) border. Top with the spinach. Place another pasta square on top, drizzle with oil, then sprinkle with the parmesan. Season.

BLUE CHEESE AND WALNUT LASAGNETTE

375 g (12 oz) lasagnette

100 g (3½ oz/1 cup) walnuts

2 tablespoons butter

3 french shallots, finely choped

1 tablespoon brandy

250 ml (8 fl oz/1 cup) crème fraîche or sour cream

200 g (6½ oz) mild gorgonzola cheese, crumbled

75 g (2½ oz) baby English spinach

1 Preheat the oven to 200°C (400°F/Gas 6).

2 Cook the pasta in a large saucepan of boiling salted water until just tender. Drain well and return to pan to keep warm.

3 Meanwhile, put the walnuts on a baking tray and roast for 5 minutes, or until golden and toasted. Cool, then roughly chop.

4 Heat the butter in a large saucepan over medium heat. Add the shallots and cook for 1–2 minutes, or until soft.

5 Add the brandy and simmer for 1 minute, then stir in the crème fraîche and gorgonzola. Cook for 3–4 minutes, or until the cheese has melted and the sauce has thickened.

6 Stir in the spinach and toasted walnuts, reserving 1 tablespoon for garnish. Heat gently until the spinach has just wilted. Season.

7 Gently mix the sauce through the pasta. Serve sprinkled with the reserved walnuts.

GENOVESE PESTO SAUCE

SERVES 4

pesto (see recipe on page 8), or ready-made

500 g (1 lb 2 oz) trenette

175 g (6 oz) green beans, trimmed

175 g (6 oz) small potatoes, very thinly sliced

extra parmesan cheese, finely grated, to serve

1 **Bring a large saucepan** of salted water to the boil. Add the pasta, green beans and potatoes, stirring well to prevent the pasta from sticking together. Cook until the pasta is just tender (the vegetables should be cooked by this time), then drain, reserving a little of the water.

2 **Return the pasta** and vegetables to the saucepan, add the pesto, and mix well. If necessary, add some of the reserved water to loosen the pasta. Season and serve immediately with the extra parmesan.

RAVIOLI WITH ROASTED RED CAPSICUM SAUCE

SERVES 4

6 red capsicums (peppers)
625 g (1 lb 6 oz) ravioli
2 tablespoons olive oil
3 garlic cloves, crushed
2 leeks, thinly sliced
1 tablespoon chopped oregano
2 teaspoons soft brown sugar
250 ml (9 fl oz/1 cup) vegetable stock

1 **Cut the capsicum** into large flattish pieces and remove the membrane and seeds. Cook, skin side up, under a hot grill (broiler) until the skin blackens and blisters. Cool in a plastic bag, then peel the skin.

2 **Cook the pasta** in a large saucepan of boiling salted water until just tender. Drain well and return to the pan to keep warm.

3 **Meanwhile,** heat the olive oil in a frying pan over medium heat. Cook the garlic and leek for 3–4 minutes, or until softened. Add the oregano and brown sugar and stir for 1 minute.

4 **Place the capsicum** and leek mixture in a food processor or blender, season and process until combined. Add the stock and process until smooth.

5 **Gently toss** the sauce through the pasta over low heat until warmed through.

SPINACH AND RICOTTA GNOCCHI

SERVES 4

4 slices white bread

125 ml (4 fl oz/½ cup) milk

500 g (1 lb/2 oz) frozen spinach, thawed

250 g (9 oz) ricotta cheese

2 eggs

60 g (2¼ oz) parmesan cheese, grated

30 g (1 oz/¼ cup) plain (all-purpose) flour

parmesan shavings, to serve

GARLIC BUTTER SAUCE

100 g (3½ oz) butter

2 garlic cloves, crushed

3 tablespoons chopped fresh basil

1 ripe tomato, diced

1 **Remove the crusts** from the bread and soak in the milk in a shallow dish for 10 minutes. Squeeze out any excess milk from the bread.

2 **Squeeze out** any excess liquid from the spinach.

3 **Place the bread**, spinach, ricotta, eggs and parmesan in a bowl and mix thoroughly. Refrigerate, covered, for 1 hour.

4 **Remove the mixture** from the refrigerator and fold the flour in well. Lightly dust your hands in flour and roll heaped teaspoons of the mixture into dumplings. Lower batches of the gnocchi into a large saucepan of boiling salted water. Cook for about 2 minutes, or until the gnocchi rise to the surface. Transfer to a serving plate and keep warm.

5 **To make the sauce**, combine all the ingredients in a small saucepan and cook over medium heat for 3 minutes, or until the butter is nutty brown.

6 **Drizzle over the gnocchi** and sprinkle with the shaved parmesan.

PASTA SHELLS WITH WALNUT PESTO

SERVES 4

125 g (4 oz) day-old crusty bread, crusts removed

185 g (6 oz/1½ cups) walnut pieces

500 g (1 lb 2 oz) pasta shells

1 very large handful fresh basil, roughly chopped

2–3 garlic cloves, peeled

1 small fresh red chilli, seeded and roughly chopped

½ teaspoon finely grated lemon zest

60 ml (2 fl oz/¼ cup) lemon juice

125 ml (4 fl oz/½ cup) olive oil

1 Preheat the oven to 160°C (315°F/Gas 2–3). Cut the bread into 2 cm (¾ inch) thick slices and place on a baking tray with the walnuts. Bake for 8–10 minutes, or until the bread is dried out a little and the walnuts are lightly toasted. Don't overcook the walnuts or they will become bitter.

2 Meanwhile, cook the pasta in a large pan of rapidly boiling salted water until just tender. Drain and return to the pan to keep warm.

3 Break the bread into chunks and mix in a food processor with the walnuts, basil, garlic, chilli, lemon zest and juice. Use the pulse button to chop the mixture without forming a paste. Transfer to a bowl and stir in the oil.

4 Toss through the pasta, then season to taste with salt and pepper.

COTELLI WITH CAPERS, BOCCONCINI AND BASIL OIL

SERVES 4

125 ml (4 fl oz/½ cup) olive oil

125 g (4 oz) jar capers in brine, drained

500 g (1 lb/2 oz) cotelli

2 tablespoons lemon juice

5 large handfuls fresh basil

35 g (1 oz/⅓ cup) grated parmesan
   cheese

250 g (9 oz) cherry tomatoes, quartered

8 bocconcini (fresh baby mozzarella
   cheese), quartered

extra virgin olive oil, for serving

1 **Heat half the olive oil** in a pan, add the capers and cook over high heat for 3–4 minutes, or until crisp and golden. Drain on paper towels and set aside.

2 **Cook pasta** in a large pan of rapidly boiling salted water until just tender. Drain and return to the pan to keep warm.

3 **Meanwhile,** mix the lemon juice, 3 large handfuls of the basil and the remaining olive oil in a food processor until smooth. Season.

4 **Roughly tear** the remaining basil leaves, then toss through the warm pasta with the basil mixture, 2 tablespoons of the parmesan and the cherry tomatoes.

5 **Spoon into warmed bowls** and top with the bocconcini and capers. Drizzle with extra virgin olive oil and garnish with the remaining grated parmesan. Serve immediately.

RICH CHEESE MACARONI

SERVES 4–6

450 g (1 lb) elbow macaroni

40 g (1½ oz) butter

300 ml (10½ fl oz) cream

125 g (4½ oz) fontina cheese, sliced

125 g (4½ oz) provolone cheese, grated

100 g (3½ oz) gruyère cheese, grated

125 g (4½ oz) blue castello cheese, crumbled

40 g (½ cup) fresh white breadcrumbs

25 g (1½ oz/¼ cup) grated parmesan cheese

1 Preheat the oven to 180°C (350°F/Gas 4). Cook the pasta in a large saucepan of boiling salted water until just tender. Drain and keep warm.

2 Melt half the butter in a large saucepan. Add the cream and, when just coming to the boil, add the fontina, provolone, gruyère and blue castello cheeses, stirring constantly over low heat for 3 minutes, or until melted. Season with salt and ground white pepper.

3 Add the pasta to the cheese mixture and mix well.

4 Spoon the mixture into a greased shallow 2 litre (8 cup) ovenproof dish. Sprinkle with the breadcrumbs mixed with the parmesan, dot with the remaining cubed butter and bake for 25 minutes, or until the top is golden and crisp. Serve with a mixed green salad.

PASTA PRONTO

SERVES 4

2 tablespoons extra virgin olive oil

4 garlic cloves, finely chopped

1 small red chilli, finely chopped

3 x 400 g (14 oz) tins chopped tomatoes

1 teaspoon sugar

80 ml (2½ fl oz/⅓ cup) dry white wine

3 tablespoons chopped herbs such as basil or parsley

400 g (14 oz) vermicelli (see Note)

35 g (1¼ oz/⅓ cup) shaved parmesan cheese

1 **Heat the oil** in a large deep frying pan and cook the garlic and chilli for 1 minute.

2 **Add the tomato,** sugar, wine, herbs and 440 ml (15¼ fl oz/1¾ cups) water. Bring to the boil and season.

3 **Reduce the heat** to medium and add the pasta, breaking the strands if they are too long. Cook for 10 minutes, or until the pasta is cooked, stirring often to stop the pasta from sticking. The pasta will thicken the sauce as it cooks.

4 **Season to taste** and serve in bowls with shaved parmesan.

Note: Vermicelli is a pasta similar to spaghetti, but thinner. You can also use spaghettini or angel hair pasta for this recipe.

FETTUCINE WITH SWEET POTATO, FETA AND OLIVES

SERVES 4–6

1.5 kg (3 lb/5 oz) orange sweet potato, cut into small cubes

80 ml (2¾ fl oz/⅓ cup) olive oil

4 garlic clove, crushed

2 tablespoons butter

4 red onions, sliced into thin wedges

500 g (1 lb/2 oz) fresh basil fettucine

400 g (14 oz/2¾ cups) soft feta cheese, diced

200 g (7 oz/1½ cups) small black olives

1 very large handful fresh basil, torn

extra virgin olive oil, to drizzle

1 **Preheat the oven** to 200°C (400°F/Gas 6).

2 **Place the sweet potato,** oil and garlic in a bowl and toss to coat the sweet potato. Lay out the sweet potato in a roasting tin and roast for 15 minutes. Turn and roast for another 15 minutes, until tender and golden — make sure the sweet potato is not too soft or it will not hold its shape. Keep warm.

3 **Meanwhile,** melt the butter in a deep frying pan and cook the onion over low heat, stirring occasionally, for 25–30 minutes, or until soft and slightly caramelised.

4 **Cook the pasta** in a large pan of rapidly boiling salted water until just tender. Drain and return to the pan.

5 **Add the onion** to the pasta and toss together. Add the sweet potato, feta, olives and basil and gently toss.

6 **Serve** drizzled with extra virgin olive oil.

CAVATELLI WITH HERB SAUCE AND PECORINO

SERVES 4

400 g (14 oz) cavatelli

90 g (3¼ oz) butter

2 garlic cloves, crushed

3 tablespoons snipped fresh chives

3 tablespoons shredded fresh basil

1 tablespoon shredded fresh sage

1 teaspoon fresh thyme

60 ml (2 fl oz/¼ cup) warm vegetable stock

60 g (2 oz) pecorino cheese, grated (see Note)

1 **Cook the pasta** in a large pan of rapidly boiling salted water until al dente. Drain and return to the pan to keep warm.

2 **Meanwhile,** heat the butter in a small saucepan over medium heat, add the garlic and cook for 1 minute, or until fragrant.

3 **Add the chives,** basil, sage and thyme and cook for a further minute.

4 **Add the herb mixture** and stock to the pasta in the pan. Return to the heat for 2–3 minutes, or until warmed through. Season to taste, add the Pecorino and stir well.

5 **Divide among bowls** and garnish with sage leaves.

Note: Pecorino is Italian sheep's milk cheese with a sharp flavour. If you can't find it, use parmesan instead.

PENNE WITH RUSTIC LENTIL SAUCE

SERVES 4–6

1 litre vegetable stock
350 g (35 fl oz/4 cups) penne
80 ml (2½ fl oz/⅓ cup) virgin olive oil, plus extra for serving
1 onion, chopped
2 carrots, diced
3 celery stalks, diced
3 garlic cloves, crushed
1 tablespoon plus 1 teaspoon chopped fresh thyme
400 g (14 oz) tin lentils, drained

1 Boil the stock in a large saucepan for 10 minutes, or until reduced by half.

2 Meanwhile, cook the pasta in a large pan of rapidly boiling salted water until just tender. Drain well and toss with 2 tablespoons of the olive oil.

3 Heat the remaining oil in a large, deep frying pan, add the onion, carrot and celery and cook over medium heat for 10 minutes, or until browned.

4 Add two-thirds of the crushed garlic and 1 tablespoon of the thyme and cook for a further 1 minute.

5 Add the stock, bring to the boil and cook for 8 minutes, or until tender.

6 Stir in the lentils and heat through.

7 Stir in the remaining garlic and thyme and season well — the stock should be slightly syrupy at this point.

8 Combine the pasta with the lentil sauce in a large bowl and drizzle with virgin olive oil to serve.

PASTA PRIMAVERA

SERVES 4

120 g (4 oz) broad (fava) beans, fresh or frozen

150 g (6 oz) asparagus, cut into short lengths

350 g (12 oz) fresh tagliatelle

100 g (3½ oz/¾ cup) green beans, cut into short lengths

120 g (4½ oz/¾ cup) peas, fresh or frozen

30 g (1 oz) butter

1 small fennel bulb, thinly sliced

375 ml (13 fl oz/1½ cups) thick (double/ heavy) cream

2 tablespoons grated parmesan cheese, plus extra, to serve

1 **Bring a large saucepan** of water to the boil. Add 1 teaspoon of salt, the broad beans and asparagus and simmer for 3 minutes. Remove the vegetables with a slotted spoon and set them aside.

2 **Add the tagliatelle** to the saucepan and, when it has softened, stir in the beans and the peas (if you're using frozen peas, add them a few minutes later). Cook for about 4 minutes, or until the pasta is just tender.

3 **Meanwhile,** heat the butter in a large frying pan. Add the fennel and cook over moderately low heat without colouring for 5 minutes. Add the cream, season with salt and pepper and cook at a low simmer.

4 **Peel the skins** from the broad beans (to give them a bright green appearance in the finished dish).

5 **Drain the pasta,** green beans and peas and add them to the frying pan.

6 **Add 2 tablespoons** of parmesan and the broad beans and asparagus. Toss lightly to coat. Serve immediately with extra parmesan.

PASTA WITH GRILLED CAPSICUM

SERVES 4–6

6 large red capsicums (peppers), halved

400 g (14 oz) pasta gnocchi

2 tablespoons olive oil

1 onion, thinly sliced

3 garlic cloves, finely chopped

2 tablespoons shredded basil leaves

whole basil leaves, to garnish

shaved parmesan cheese, to serve

1 **Cut the capsicums** into large flattish pieces. Cook, skin side up, under a hot grill (broiler) until the skin blackens and blisters. Place in a plastic bag and leave to cool, then peel the skin.

2 **Cook the pasta** in a saucepan of boiling salted water until just tender.

3 **Meanwhile,** heat the oil in a large frying pan, add the onion and garlic and cook over medium heat for 5 minutes, or until soft. Cut one capsicum into thin strips and add to the onion mixture.

4 **Chop the remaining capsicum,** then purée in a food processor until smooth. Add to the onion mixture and cook over low heat for 5 minutes, or until warmed through.

5 **Toss the sauce** through the hot pasta. Season, then stir in the shredded basil. Garnish with the basil leaves and serve with the parmesan.

CHICKEN

CREAMY PESTO CHICKEN PENNE

SERVES 4

1 tablespoon oil

40 g (1½ oz) butter

400 g (14 oz) boneless, skinless chicken
  breast

170 g (6 oz) thin asparagus, cut into
  4 cm (1½ inch) lengths

3 spring onions (scallions), chopped

4 garlic cloves, crushed

300 g (10½ oz) sour cream

125 ml (4 fl oz/½ cup) pouring cream

185 ml (6 fl oz/¾ cup) chicken stock

100 g (3½ oz/1 cup) grated parmesan
  cheese

30 g (1 oz) finely chopped basil

2 tablespoons toasted pine nuts

400 g (14 oz) penne

basil leaves, to garnish

pesto, for garnish (see recipe on page 8),
  or ready-made

1 Heat the oil and half the butter in a large frying pan over high heat. Add the chicken and cook for 5 minutes on each side, or until just cooked. Remove, cover and cool, then cut into 1 cm (½ inch) slices.

2 Add the asparagus and spring onion to the pan and cook for 2 minutes, or until the asparagus is just tender. Remove. Wipe the pan with paper towels.

3 Reduce the heat to medium and add the remaining butter and the garlic. Cook for 2 minutes, or until golden brown.

4 Add the sour cream, cream and stock, and simmer for 10 minutes or until reduced slightly.

5 Add the parmesan and basil and stir for 2 minutes, or until the cheese has melted. Return the chicken and asparagus to the pan. Add the pine nuts and cook for 2 minutes to heat through. Season.

6 Meanwhile, cook the pasta in a large saucepan of boiling salted water until just tender. Drain well and return to pan to keep warm. Combine the sauce and the pasta. Garnish with basil leaves.

CHICKEN RAVIOLI WITH BUTTERED SAGE SAUCE

SERVES 4

500 g (1 lb 2 oz) fresh or dried chicken-filled ravioli or agnolotti

60 g (2 oz) butter

4 spring onions, chopped

2 tablespoons fresh sage, chopped

salt and pepper, to taste

60 g (2 oz/½ cup) freshly grated parmesan cheese, for serving

fresh sage leaves, extra, for garnish

1 Add the ravioli to a large pan of rapidly boiling water and cook until just tender. Drain the pasta in a colander and return to the pan. To test whether the ravioli is done – take a piece and bite through.

2 While the ravioli is cooking, melt the butter in a heavy-based pan. Add the spring onion and sage and stir for 2 minutes. Add the salt and pepper.

3 Add the sauce to the pasta and toss well.

4 To serve, pour onto a warmed serving platter and sprinkle with the parmesan. Garnish with fresh sage leaves and serve immediately.

CHILLI LINGUINE WITH CHERMOULA CHICKEN

SERVES 4

600 g (1 lb 5 oz) boneless, skinless
  chicken breast

500 g (1 lb 2 oz) chilli linguine

CHERMOULA

100 g (3½ oz) coriander (cilantro) leaves,
  chopped

60 g (2¼ oz) flat-leaf (Italian) parsley
  leaves, chopped

4 garlic cloves, crushed

2 teaspoons ground cumin

2 teaspoons ground paprika

125 ml (4 fl oz/½ cup) lemon juice

2 teaspoons lemon zest

100 ml (3½ fl oz) olive oil

1 **Heat a large non-stick** frying pan over medium heat. Add the chicken breasts and cook until tender. Remove from the pan and leave for 5 minutes before cutting into thin slices.

2 **Cook the pasta** in a large saucepan of boiling salted water until just tender. Drain well and return to the pan to keep warm.

3 **Meanwhile,** combine the chermoula ingredients in a bowl and add the sliced chicken. Serve the pasta topped with the chermoula chicken.

BAVETTE WITH CHICKEN, PINE NUTS AND LEMON

SERVES 4–6

1.3 kg (3 lb) chicken
1 garlic bulb, cloves separated and left unpeeled
3 tablespoons olive oil
30 g (1 oz) butter, softened
1 tablespoon finely chopped thyme
125 ml (4 fl oz/½ cup) lemon juice
500 g (1 lb 2 oz) bavette or spaghetti
2 tablespoons currants
1 teaspoon finely grated lemon zest
50 g (1¾ oz/⅓ cup) pine nuts, toasted
1 very large handful finely chopped flat-leaf (Italian) parsley

1 Preheat the oven to 200°C (400°F/Gas 6). Remove the neck from the inside of the chicken and place the neck in a roasting tin. Rinse the inside of the chicken with cold water. Insert the garlic cloves into the cavity, then put the chicken in the tin.

2 Combine the oil, butter, thyme and lemon juice, then rub over the chicken. Season. Roast for 1 hour, or until the skin is golden and the juices run clear when the thigh is pierced with a skewer. Transfer the chicken to a bowl. Remove the garlic from the cavity, cool, then squeeze the garlic cloves out of their skins and finely chop.

3 Cook the pasta in a large saucepan of boiling salted water until just tender. Drain well and return to the pan to keep warm.

4 Meanwhile, pour the juices from the roasting tin into a saucepan and discard the neck. Add the currants, zest and chopped garlic, then simmer over low heat. Remove all the meat from the chicken and shred. Add the resting juices to the pan. Add the chicken, pine nuts, parsley and sauce to the pasta and toss.

FUSILLI WITH CHICKEN, MUSHROOM AND TARRAGON

SERVES 4

375 g (13 oz) fusilli

2 tablespoons olive oil

350 g (12 oz) chicken tenderloins, cut into 2 cm (¾ inch) pieces

20 g (¾ oz) butter

400 g (14 oz) Swiss brown or button mushrooms, sliced

2 garlic cloves, finely chopped

125 ml (4 fl oz/½ cup) dry white wine

185 ml (6 fl oz/¾ cup) pouring cream

1 teaspoon finely grated lemon zest

2 tablespoons lemon juice

1 tablespoon chopped tarragon

2 tablespoons chopped flat-leaf (Italian) parsley

25 g (1 oz/¼ cup) grated parmesan cheese, plus extra, to serve

1 Cook the pasta in a large saucepan of boiling salted water until just tender. Drain well and return to the pan to keep warm.

2 Meanwhile, heat 1 tablespoon of the oil in a large frying pan over high heat. Add the chicken and cook for 3–4 minutes, or until lightly browned. Remove from the pan.

3 Heat the butter and the remaining oil in the frying pan over high heat. Add the mushrooms and cook for 3 minutes. Add the garlic and cook for a further 2 minutes.

4 Pour in the wine, then reduce the heat to low and simmer for 5 minutes.

5 Add the cream and chicken and simmer for about 5 minutes, or until thickened.

6 Stir in the lemon zest, lemon juice, tarragon, parsley and parmesan. Season, then add the pasta, tossing until well combined. Serve with the extra parmesan.

LASAGNETTE WITH SPICY CHICKEN MEATBALLS

SERVES 4

750 g (1 lb 10 oz) minced (ground) chicken

2 tablespoons chopped coriander (cilantro) leaves

1½ tablespoons red curry paste

2 tablespoons oil

1 red onion, finely chopped

3 garlic cloves, crushed

875 g (1 lb 15 oz/3½ cups) ready-made tomato pasta sauce

2 teaspoons soft brown sugar

350 g (12 oz) lasagnette

1 **Line a tray** with baking paper. Combine the meat, coriander and 1 tablespoon of the curry paste. Roll heaped tablespoons of the mixture into balls and put on the tray. Refrigerate.

2 **Heat the oil** in a large deep frying pan over medium heat. Cook the onion and garlic for 2–3 minutes, or until softened.

3 **Add the remaining curry paste** and cook, stirring, for 1 minute, or until fragrant.

4 **Add the pasta sauce** and sugar and stir well. Reduce the heat and add the meatballs. Cook, turning halfway through, for 10 minutes, or until the meatballs are cooked through.

5 **Meanwhile,** cook the pasta in a large saucepan of boiling salted water until just tender. Drain well and return to the pan to keep warm.

6 **Serve** topped with the sauce and meatballs. Garnish with coriander, if desired.

STRACCI WITH ARTICHOKES AND CHARGRILLED CHICKEN

SERVES 6

1 tablespoon olive oil

3 boneless, skinless chicken breasts

500 g (1 lb 2 oz) stracci

8 slices prosciutto

280 g (10 oz) jar artichokes in oil,
    drained and quartered, oil reserved

150 g (5½ oz) semi-dried (sun-blushed)
    tomatoes, thinly sliced

80 g (2¾ oz) baby rocket (arugula)

2–3 tablespoons balsamic vinegar

1   Lightly brush a frying or chargrill pan with the oil and heat over high heat. Cook the chicken for 6–8 minutes each side, or until cooked through. Cut into thin slices on the diagonal.

2   Meanwhile, cook the pasta in a large saucepan of boiling salted water until just tender. Drain well and return to the pan to keep warm.

3   Put the prosciutto on a lined baking tray and cook under a hot grill (broiler) for 2 minutes each side, or until crisp. Cool slightly and break into pieces.

4   In a bowl, combine the pasta with the chicken, prosciutto, artichokes, tomato and rocket and toss.

5   Whisk together 3 tablespoons of the reserved artichoke oil and the balsamic vinegar and toss through the pasta mixture. Season and serve.

CREAMY CHICKEN AND PEPPERCORN PAPPARDELLE

SERVES 4

2 boneless, skinless chicken breasts

30 g (1 oz) butter

1 onion, halved and thinly sliced

2 tablespoons drained green peppercorns, slightly crushed

125 ml (4 fl oz/½ cup) white wine

300 ml (10½ fl oz) pouring (whipping) cream

400 g (14 oz) fresh pappardelle

80 g (2¾ oz/⅓ cup) sour cream (optional)

2 tablespoons snipped chives

1 **Cut the chicken** in half so that you have four flat fillets and season.

2 **Melt the butter** in a frying pan over medium heat. Add the chicken and cook for 3 minutes on each side, or until lightly browned and cooked through. Remove from the pan, cut into slices and keep warm.

3 **Add the onion** and peppercorns to the same pan and cook over medium heat for 3 minutes, or until the onion has softened slightly.

4 **Add the wine** and cook for 1 minute, or until reduced by half. Stir in the cream and cook for 4–5 minutes, or until thickened slightly, then season.

5 **Meanwhile,** cook the pasta in a large saucepan of boiling salted water until just tender. Drain well and return to the pan to keep warm.

6 **Combine the pasta,** chicken and any juices and cream sauce. Serve topped with sour cream, sprinkled with chives.

CHICKEN, BROCCOLI AND PASTA BAKE

SERVES 4

300 g (10½ oz) fusilli

425 g (15 oz) tinned cream of mushroom soup

2 eggs

185 g (6½ oz/¾ cup) whole-egg mayonnaise

1 tablespoon dijon mustard

210 g (7½ oz/1⅔ cups) grated cheddar cheese

600 g (1 lb 5 oz) boneless, skinless chicken breast, thinly sliced

400 g (14 oz) frozen broccoli pieces, thawed

40 g (1½ oz/½ cup) fresh breadcrumbs

1 **Preheat the oven** to 180°C (350°F/Gas 4). Cook the pasta in a large saucepan of boiling salted water until just tender. Drain well and return to the pan to keep warm.

2 **Combine the soup,** eggs, mayonnaise, mustard and half the cheese in a bowl.

3 **Heat a lightly greased** non-stick frying pan over medium heat. Add the chicken pieces and cook for 5–6 minutes, or until cooked through. Season, then set aside to cool.

4 **Add the chicken** and broccoli to the pasta. Pour the soup mixture over the top and stir until well combined.

5 **Transfer the mixture** to a 3 litre (105 fl oz/12 cup) ovenproof dish. Sprinkle with the combined breadcrumbs and remaining cheese. Bake for 20 minutes, or until the top is golden brown.

CHICKEN CARBONARA

SERVES 4

500 g (1 lb 2oz) fresh tomato fettucine

600 g (1 lb 5 oz) chicken tenderloins

40 g (1½ oz) butter

3 eggs

300 ml (10½ fl oz) pouring cream

50 g (1¾ oz/½ cup) grated parmesan

shaved parmesan and fresh basil leaves, to garnish

1 Cook pasta in a large pan of rapidly boiling salted water until just tender. Drain and return to the pan to keep warm.

2 **Trim and slice** the tenderloins in half on the diagonal. Melt the butter in a frying pan and cook the chicken for 4–5 minutes, or until browned.

3 **Lightly beat the eggs** and cream together and stir in the grated parmesan. Season with salt to taste and stir through the chicken.

4 **Combine the chicken** and cream mixture with the fettucine in the frying pan. Reduce the heat and cook, stirring constantly, for 10–15 seconds, or until the sauce is slightly thickened. Do not keep on the heat too long or the eggs will set and scramble. Season with black pepper and serve, garnished with the extra parmesan and basil leaves.

CHICKEN AND EGGPLANT PASTA

SERVES 4

375 g (12 oz) penne

100 ml (3½ fl oz) olive oil

4 slender eggplants, thinly sliced on the diagonal

2 chicken breast fillets

2 teaspoons lemon juice

15 g (½ oz/½ cup) chopped fresh flat-leaf (Italian) parsley

270 g (9 oz) chargrilled red capsicum, drained and sliced (see Note)

150 g (5 oz) fresh asparagus, trimmed, blanched and cut into short lengths

90 g (3 oz) semi-dried tomatoes, finely sliced

1   Cook the pasta in a large pan of rapidly boiling salted water until al dente. Drain and return to the pan to keep warm.

2   Meanwhile, heat 2 tablespoons of the oil in a large frying pan over high heat and cook the eggplant for 4–5 minutes, or until golden and cooked through.

3   Heat a lightly oiled chargrill pan over high heat and cook the chicken for 5 minutes each side, or until browned and cooked through. Cut into thick slices.

4   Combine the lemon juice, parsley and the remaining oil in a small jar and shake well.

5   Return the pasta to the heat, toss through the dressing, chicken, eggplant, capsicum, asparagus and tomato until well mixed and warmed through. Season with black pepper.

6   Serve warm with a little grated Parmesan.

CHICKEN TORTELLINI WITH TOMATO SAUCE

PASTA

2 cups (250 g/8 oz) plain flour

3 eggs

1 tablespoon olive oil

FILLING

20 g (¾ oz) butter

80 g (2¾ oz) chicken breast fillet, cubed

2 slices pancetta, chopped

50 g (1¾ oz/½ cup) grated parmesan

½ teaspoon nutmeg

1 egg, lightly beaten

TOMATO SAUCE

80 ml (2¾ fl oz/⅓ cup) olive oil

1.5 kg (3 lb) ripe tomatoes, peeled and chopped (see Note)

7 g (¼ oz/¼ cup) chopped fresh oregano

50 g (1¾ oz/½ cup) grated parmesan

100 g (3½ oz) fresh bocconcini, thinly sliced, to serve

1 **To make the pasta,** sift the flour and a pinch of salt into a bowl and make a well in the centre. In a jug, whisk together the eggs, oil and 1 tablespoon water. Add the egg mixture gradually to the flour, mixing to a firm dough. Gather together into a ball, adding a little extra water if necessary. Knead on a lightly floured surface for 5 minutes, or until the dough is smooth and elastic. Place in a lightly oiled bowl, cover with plastic wrap and leave for 30 minutes.

2 **To make the filling,** heat the butter in a frying pan, add the chicken and cook until golden brown, then drain. Process the chicken and pancetta in a food processor or mincer until finely chopped. Transfer to a bowl. Add cheese, nutmeg, egg and salt and pepper, to taste. Set aside.

3 **Roll out the dough** very thinly on a lightly floured surface. Using a floured cutter, cut into 5 cm (2 inch) rounds. Spoon about ½ teaspoon of filling into the centre of each round.

Fold the rounds in half to form semicircles, pressing the edges together firmly. Wrap each semicircle around your finger to form a ring and then press the ends of the dough together.

4 **To make tomato sauce,** place the oil, tomato and oregano in a frying pan and cook over high heat for 10 minutes. Stir in the parmesan, then set aside.

5 **Cook the tortellini** in two batches in a large pan of rapidly boiling water for about 6 minutes each batch, or until just tender. Drain well and return to the pan.

6 **Reheat the tomato sauce,** add to the tortellini and toss well. Divide the tortellini among individual bowls, top with the bocconcini and allow the cheese to melt a little before serving.

Note: If using pre-made tortellini you will need 500 g (1 lb 2 oz).

MEAT

FARFALLE WITH SPINACH AND BACON

SERVES 4

400 g (14 oz) farfalle

2 tablespoons extra virgin olive oil

250 g (9 oz) bacon, chopped

1 red onion, finely chopped

250 g (9 oz/5 cups) baby English
  spinach leaves, stalks trimmed

1–2 tablespoons sweet chilli sauce
  (optional)

35 g (1¼ oz/¼ cup) crumbled goat's
  cheese

1 Cook the pasta in a large saucepan of boiling salted water until just tender. Drain well and return to the pan to keep warm.

2 Meanwhile, heat the oil in a frying pan over medium heat. Add the bacon and cook for 3 minutes, or until golden.

3 Add the onion and cook for a further 4 minutes, or until softened. Toss the spinach leaves through the onion and bacon mixture for 30 seconds, or until just wilted.

4 Add the bacon and spinach mixture to the pasta, then stir in the sweet chilli sauce, if using. Season and toss well. Scatter with the crumbled goat's cheese to serve.

MUSHROOM, PANCETTA AND MOZZARELLA ORECCHIETTE

SERVES 4

400 g (14 oz) orecchiette
2 tablespoons olive oil
150 g (5½ oz) sliced pancetta, cut into short thin strips
200 g (7 oz) button mushrooms, sliced
2 leeks, sliced
250 ml (9 fl oz/1 cup) pouring cream
200 g (7 oz) smoked mozzarella (mozzarella affumicata), cut into 1 cm (½ inch) cubes
8 basil leaves, torn

1 Cook the pasta in a large saucepan of boiling salted water until just tender. Drain well and return to the pan to keep warm.

2 Meanwhile, heat the oil in a large frying pan over medium–high heat. Add the pancetta, mushrooms and leek and sauté for 5 minutes.

3 Stir in the cream and season with pepper. Simmer over low heat for 5 minutes. Stir in the pasta. Add the mozzarella and basil and toss.

TORTELLINI BOSCAIOLA

SERVES 4–6

30 g (1 oz) butter

4 bacon slices, diced

2 garlic cloves, finely chopped

300 g (10½ oz) Swiss brown or button mushrooms, sliced

60 ml (2 fl oz/¼ cup) dry white wine

375 ml (13 fl oz/1½ cups) pouring cream

1 teaspoon chopped thyme

500 g (1 lb 2 oz) veal tortellini

50 g (1¾ oz/½ cup) grated parmesan cheese

1 tablespoon chopped flat-leaf (Italian) parsley

1 **Melt the butter** in a large frying pan, add the bacon and cook over medium heat for 5 minutes, or until crisp.

2 **Add the garlic** and cook for 2 minutes, then add the mushrooms, cooking for a further 8 minutes, or until softened.

3 **Stir in the wine** and cream and add the thyme and bring to the boil. Reduce the heat to low and simmer for 10 minutes, or until the sauce has thickened.

4 **Meanwhile,** cook the pasta in a large saucepan of boiling salted water until just tender.

5 **Combine the sauce** with the hot pasta, parmesan and parsley. Season to taste and serve immediately.

PENNE WITH VEAL RAGOUT

SERVES 4

2 onions, sliced
2 bay leaves, crushed
1.5 kg (3 lb 5 oz) veal shin, cut into osso buco pieces (see Note)
250 ml (9 fl oz/1 cup) red wine
2 x 400 g (14 oz) tins chopped tomatoes
375 ml (13 fl oz/1½ cups) beef stock
2 teaspoons chopped fresh rosemary
400 g (14 oz) penne
150 g (5½ oz/1 cup) frozen peas

1 Preheat the oven to 220°C (425°F/Gas 7). Scatter the onion over the bottom of a large roasting tin, lightly spray with oil and place the bay leaves and veal pieces on top. Season with salt and pepper. Roast for 10–15 minutes, or until the veal is browned. Take care that the onion doesn't burn.

2 Pour the wine over the veal and return to the oven for a further 5 minutes. Reduce the heat to 180°C (350°F/Gas 4), remove the tin from the oven and pour on the tomato, stock and 1 teaspoon of the rosemary. Cover with foil and return to the oven. Cook for 2 hours, or until the veal is starting to fall from the bone. Remove the foil and cook for a further 15 minutes, or until the meat loosens away from the bone and the liquid has evaporated slightly.

3 Cook the pasta in a large pan of rapidly boiling salted water until just tender. Drain and return to the pan to keep warm.

4 Meanwhile, remove the veal from the oven and cool slightly. Add the peas and remaining rosemary and place over a hotplate. Cook over medium heat for 5 minutes, or until the peas are cooked. Serve the pasta topped with the ragout.

Note: Most butchers sell veal shin cut into osso buco pieces. If sold in a whole piece, ask the butcher to cut it for you (the pieces are about 3–4 cm [1¼–1½ in] thick). It is also available at some supermarkets. You can either remove the meat from the bone before serving, or leave it on.

PENNE WITH PORK AND FENNEL SAUSAGES

SERVES 4

6 Italian pork and fennel sausages
  (about 550 g/1 lb 4 oz)

1 tablespoon olive oil

1 small red onion, finely chopped

2–3 garlic cloves, crushed

½ teaspoon chilli flakes

300 g (10½ oz) field or button
  mushrooms, thinly sliced

800 g (1 lb 12 oz) tinned chopped
  tomatoes

1 tablespoon finely chopped thyme

500 g (1 lb 2 oz) penne rigate

grated parmesan cheese, to serve

1 Split the sausages open, remove and crumble the filling and discard the skins.

2 Heat the oil in a large saucepan over medium–high heat. Cook the onion for 3–4 minutes, or until fragrant and transparent. Add the garlic, chilli flakes, mushrooms and crumbled sausage meat. Cook over high heat, stirring gently to mash the sausage meat, for 4–5 minutes, or until the meat is evenly browned. Continue to cook, stirring once or twice, for about 10 minutes.

3 Stir in the tomato and thyme, then bring the sauce to the boil. Cover and cook over medium–low heat for 20 minutes, stirring occasionally to make sure the sauce doesn't stick to the bottom of the pan.

4 Meanwhile, cook the pasta in a large saucepan of boiling salted water until just tender. Drain well and return to the pan to keep warm.

5 Add the pasta to the sauce and stir to combine. Serve with the parmesan.

MACARONI CHEESE WITH PANCETTA

SERVES 4

390 g (13¾ oz/2½ cups) macaroni

75 g (2½ oz) pancetta, diced

500 ml (17 fl oz/2 cups) pouring cream

125 g (4½ oz/1 cup) grated cheddar cheese

260 g (9¼ oz/2 cups) grated gruyère cheese

100 g (3½ oz/1 cup) grated parmesan cheese

1 garlic clove, crushed

2 teaspoons dijon mustard

½ teaspoon paprika

2 tablespoons snipped chives, plus extra to garnish

1 **Cook the pasta** in a large saucepan of boiling salted water until just tender. Drain well and return to the pan to keep warm.

2 **Meanwhile,** cook the pancetta in a large saucepan over high heat, stirring, for 4 minutes or until well browned and slightly crisp. Drain on paper towel.

3 **Reduce the heat** to medium, stir in the cream and simmer. Add the cheeses, garlic, mustard and paprika. Stir for 5 minutes, or until the cheeses have melted and the sauce has thickened. Season.

4 **Add the pasta** and pancetta and stir for 1 minute, or until heated through. Stir in the chives, garnish with the extra chives and serve.

PENNE CARBONARA

SERVES 4–6

400 g (14 oz) penne

1 tablespoon olive oil

200 g (7 oz) piece pancetta or bacon, cut into long thin strips

6 egg yolks

185 ml (6 fl oz/¾ cup) pouring cream

75 g (2½ oz/¾ cup) grated parmesan cheese

1 Cook the pasta in a large saucepan of boiling salted water until just tender. Drain well and return to the pan to keep warm.

2 Meanwhile, heat the oil in a frying pan over high heat. Cook the pancetta for 6 minutes, or until crisp and golden. Remove with a slotted spoon and drain on paper towel.

3 Beat the egg yolks, cream and parmesan together in a bowl and season well.

4 Return the pasta to its saucepan and pour the egg mixture over the pasta, tossing gently. Add the pancetta and cook over very low heat for 30–60 seconds, or until the sauce thickens and coats the pasta. Season and serve immediately.

Note: Be careful not to cook the pasta over high heat once you have added the egg mixture, or the sauce risks being scrambled by the heat.

ORECCHIETTE WITH CAULIFLOWER, BACON AND PECORINO

SERVES 4

750 g (1 lb 10 oz) cauliflower, cut into florets

500 g (1 lb 2 oz) orecchiette (see Note)

125 ml (4 fl oz/½ cup) olive oil, plus extra, to drizzle

150 g (5½ oz) bacon, diced

2 garlic cloves, finely chopped

80 g (2¾ oz/½ cup) pine nuts, toasted

45 g (1½ oz/½ cup) grated pecorino cheese

1 very large handful chopped flat-leaf (Italian) parsley

60 g (2¼ oz/¾ cup) fresh breadcrumbs, toasted

1   Bring a large saucepan of salted water to the boil and cook the cauliflower for 5–6 minutes, or until tender. Drain.

2   Cook the pasta in a large saucepan of boiling salted water until just tender. Drain well and return to the pan to keep warm.

3   Heat the oil in a frying pan over medium heat. Cook the bacon for 4–5 minutes, or until just crisp.

4   Add the garlic and cook for 1 minute, or until just golden. Add the cauliflower and toss well.

5   Add the pasta to the pan with the pine nuts, pecorino cheese, parsley and 40 g (1½ oz/½ cup) of the breadcrumbs and stir to combine. Season, sprinkle with the remaining breadcrumbs and drizzle with a little extra oil.

Note: Orecchiette means 'little ears' in Italian. If unavailable, use conchiglie or cavatelli.

VEAL TORTELLINI WITH CREAMY MUSHROOM SAUCE

SERVES 4

500 g (1 lb 2 oz) veal tortellini

3 tablespoons olive oil

600 g (1 lb 5 oz) Swiss brown mushrooms, thinly sliced

2 garlic cloves, crushed

125 ml (4 fl oz/½ cup) dry white wine

300 ml (10½ fl oz) thick (double/heavy) cream

pinch ground nutmeg

3 tablespoons finely chopped flat-leaf (Italian) parsley

30 g (1 oz) grated parmesan cheese

1 Cook the pasta in a large saucepan of boiling salted water until just tender. Drain well and return to the pan to keep warm.

2 Meanwhile, heat the oil in a frying pan over medium heat. Add the mushrooms and cook, stirring occasionally, for 5 minutes, or until softened.

3 Add the garlic and cook for 1 minute. Stir in the wine and cook for 5 minutes, or until the liquid has reduced by half.

4 Combine the cream, nutmeg and parsley. Add to the sauce and cook for 3–5 minutes, or until the sauce thickens slightly. Season.

5 Divide the tortellini among four serving plates and spoon over the mushroom sauce. Sprinkle with parmesan cheese.

PAPRIKA VEAL WITH CARAWAY FETTUCINE

SERVES 4

3 tablespoons oil
1 kg (2 lb 4 oz) diced veal shoulder
1 large onion, thinly sliced
3 garlic cloves, finely chopped
60 g (2¼ oz/¼ cup) paprika
½ teaspoon caraway seeds
800 g (1 lb 12 oz) tinned chopped tomatoes, half drained
350 g (12 oz) fettucine
40 g (1½ oz) butter, softened

1   Heat half the oil in a large saucepan over medium–high heat. Brown the veal in batches for 3 minutes per batch. Remove the veal from the pan and set aside with any pan juices.

2   Add the remaining oil to the pan and sauté the onion and garlic over medium heat for 5 minutes, or until softened.

3   Add the paprika and ¼ teaspoon of the caraway seeds and stir for 30 seconds.

4   Add the chopped tomatoes and their liquid plus 125 ml (4 fl oz/½ cup) water. Return the veal to the pan with any juices, increase the heat to high and bring to the boil. Reduce the heat to low, then cover and simmer for 1 hour 15 minutes, or until the meat is tender and the sauce has thickened.

5   Meanwhile, cook the pasta in a large saucepan of boiling salted water until just tender. Drain well and return to the pan to keep warm.

6   Stir in the butter and the remaining caraway seeds. Serve immediately with the veal.

SPAGHETTI WITH HERB, GARLIC AND CHILLI OIL

SERVES 4–6

250 ml (9 fl oz/ 1 cup) olive oil

2 bird's eye chillies, seeded and thinly sliced

5–6 large garlic cloves, crushed

500 g (1 lb/2 oz) spaghetti

100 g (3½ oz) thinly sliced prosciutto

2 very large handfuls chopped fresh flat-leaf (Italian) parsley

2 tablespoons chopped fresh basil

2 tablespoons chopped fresh oregano

75 g (2½ oz/¾ cup) grated parmesan cheese

1 Pour the oil into a small saucepan with the chilli and garlic. Slowly heat the oil over low heat for about 12 minutes to infuse the oil with the garlic and chilli. Don't allow the oil to reach smoking point or the garlic will burn and taste bitter.

2 Meanwhile, cook the pasta in a large pan of rapidly boiling salted water until just tender. Drain well and return to the pan to keep warm.

3 Cook the prosciutto under a hot grill for 2 minutes each side, or until crispy. Cool and break into pieces.

4 Pour the hot oil mixture over the spaghetti and toss well with the prosciutto, fresh herbs and parmesan. Season to taste.

Note: This sauce is traditionally served with spaghetti. It is simple but relies on good-quality ingredients.

HAM TORTELLINI WITH NUTTY HERB SAUCE

SERVES 4–6

500 g (1 lb 2 oz) ham and
  cheese tortellini

60 g (2¼ oz) butter

100 g (3½ oz/1 cup) walnuts, chopped

100 g (3½ oz/⅔ cup) pine nuts

2 tablespoons finely chopped flat-leaf
  (Italian) parsley

2 teaspoons chopped thyme

60 g (2¼ oz/¼ cup) ricotta cheese

60 ml (2 fl oz/¼ cup) thick (double/
  heavy) cream

1 Cook the pasta in a large saucepan of boiling water until al dente. Drain and return to the pan.

2 Meanwhile, heat the butter in a frying pan over medium heat until foaming. Add the walnuts and pine nuts and stir for 5 minutes, or until golden brown.

3 Add the parsley and thyme and season to taste.

4 Beat the ricotta and cream together. Add the nutty sauce to the pasta and toss. Divide among serving bowls and top with the ricotta cream.

ZITI CARBONARA

SERVES 4–6

1 tablespoon olive oil

200 g (7 oz) piece pancetta, cut into long thin strips

500 g (1 lb 2 oz) ziti

4 egg yolks

300 ml (10½ fl oz) pouring cream

50 g (1¾ oz/½ cup) grated parmesan cheese, plus extra to serve

2 tablespoons finely chopped flat-leaf (Italian) parsley

1 Heat the olive oil in a non-stick frying pan over high heat. Cook the pancetta for 6 minutes, or until crisp and golden.

2 Meanwhile, cook the pasta in a large saucepan of boiling salted water until just tender. Drain well and return to the pan to keep warm.

3 Beat the egg yolks, cream and parmesan together in a bowl and season. Pour over the pasta in the saucepan and toss. Add the pancetta and parsley. Cook over very low heat for 30–60 seconds, or until the sauce has thickened and coats the pasta. Don't overheat or the eggs will scramble. Season and serve with extra parmesan.

PROSCIUTTO AND VEGETABLE PASTA BAKE

SERVES 4–6

3 tablespoons olive oil

35 g (1¼ oz/⅓ cup) dry breadcrumbs

250 g (9 oz) mixed curly pasta, such as cotelli and fusilli

6 thin slices prosciutto, chopped

1 red onion, chopped

1 red capsicum (pepper), chopped

100 g (3½ oz) semi-dried (sun-blushed) tomatoes, chopped

3 tablespoons shredded basil

100 g (3½ oz/1 cup) grated parmesan cheese

4 eggs, lightly beaten

250 ml (9 fl oz/1 cup) milk

1 Preheat the oven to 180°C (350°F/Gas 4). Lightly grease a 25 cm (10 inch) round ovenproof dish. Sprinkle the dish with 2 tablespoons of the breadcrumbs to coat the base and side.

2 Cook the pasta in a large saucepan of boiling water until al dente. Drain well and return to the pan to keep warm.

3 Heat 1 tablespoon of the oil in a large frying pan over medium heat. Add the prosciutto and onion and cook for 4–5 minutes, or until softened.

4 Add the capsicum and semi-dried tomato and cook for a further 1–2 minutes.

5 Add to the pasta with the basil and parmesan and toss. Spoon into the prepared dish.

6 Place the eggs and milk in a bowl, whisk together, then season. Pour the egg mixture over the pasta. Season the remaining breadcrumbs, add the remaining oil and toss together.

7 Sprinkle the seasoned breadcrumb mixture over the pasta. Bake for 40 minutes, or until set. Cut into wedges to serve.

BEEF SAUSAGE PASTA

SERVES 4

150 g (5½ oz) spiral pasta

4 thick beef sausages

2 tablespoons olive oil

1 large red onion, cut into wedges

250 g (8 oz/1 cup) tomato pasta sauce

4 small ripe tomatoes, peeled, seeded and chopped

2 tablespoons chopped fresh flat-leaf (Italian) parsley

1 **Cook the pasta** in a large pan of rapidly boiling salted water until just tender. Drain well and return to the pan to keep warm, reserving 60 ml (2 fl oz/¼ cup) of the cooking water.

2 **Meanwhile,** prick the sausages all over with a fork. Heat a non-stick frying pan and cook the sausages over medium heat, turning often, for 5 minutes, or until cooked. Cut into thick diagonal slices and set aside.

3 **Clean the frying pan** and heat the oil. Cook the onion wedges over medium heat for 3 minutes, or until soft.

4 **Add the tomato** pasta sauce and the tomato. Cook for 5 minutes, or until the tomato has softened. Add the sliced sausage and heat through for 1 minute.

5 **Toss the pasta** through the sauce, adding a little of the reserved pasta water, if necessary. Sprinkle with parsley and serve.

LINGUINE WITH HAM, ARTICHOKE AND LEMON SAUCE

SERVES 4

500 g (1 lb 2 oz) fresh linguine

1 tablespoon butter

2 large garlic cloves, chopped

150 g (5½ oz) marinated artichokes, drained and quartered

150 g (5½ oz) sliced leg ham, cut into strips

300 ml (10 fl oz) cream

2 teaspoons roughly grated lemon rind

2 small handfuls fresh basil, torn

35 g (1¼ oz/⅓ cup) grated parmesan cheese

1 Cook the pasta in a large pan of rapidly boiling salted water until just tender. Drain and return to the pan to keep warm.

2 Meanwhile, melt the butter in a large frying pan, add the garlic and cook over medium heat for 1 minute, or until fragrant.

3 Add the artichokes and ham and cook for a further 2 minutes.

4 Add the cream and lemon zest, reduce the heat and simmer for 5 minutes, gently breaking up the artichokes with a wooden spoon.

5 Pour the sauce over the pasta, then add the basil and parmesan and toss well until the pasta is evenly coated. Serve immediately.

PENNE WITH MEATBALLS AND TOMATO

SERVES 4

MEATBALLS

2 slices white bread, crusts removed

60 ml (2 fl oz/¼ cup) milk

500 g (1 lb 2 oz) minced (ground) pork and veal (see Note)

1 small onion, finely chopped

2 garlic cloves, finely chopped

3 tablespoons finely chopped flat-leaf (Italian) parsley

2 teaspoons finely grated lemon zest

1 egg, lightly beaten

50 g (1¾ oz/½ cup) grated parmesan cheese

plain (all-purpose) flour, to coat

2 tablespoons olive oil

125 ml (4 fl oz/½ cup) white wine

2 x 420 g (14 oz) tins chopped tomatoes

1 tablespoon tomato paste (concentrated purée)

1 teaspoon caster (superfine) sugar

½ teaspoon dried oregano

500 g (1 lb 2 oz) penne rigate

oregano leaves, to garnish

1   To make the meatballs, soak the bread in the milk for 5 minutes, then squeeze out any moisture. Put the bread, mince, onion, garlic, parsley, zest, egg and parmesan in a bowl, season and mix well with your hands. Shape into walnut-size balls using damp hands, and roll lightly in the flour.

2   Heat the oil in a large deep frying pan and cook the meatballs in batches over medium heat, turning frequently, for 10 minutes, or until brown all over. Remove with a slotted spoon and drain on paper towels.

3   Pour the wine into the same frying pan and boil over medium heat for 2–3 minutes, or until it evaporates a little.

4   Add the tomato, tomato paste, sugar and dried oregano. Reduce heat. Simmer for 20 minutes to thicken the sauce.

5   Add the meatballs and simmer for 10 minutes.

6   Meanwhile, cook the pasta in a saucepan of boiling salted water until just tender.

7   To serve, divide the hot pasta among four serving plates and spoon some meatballs and sauce over the top of each. Garnish with the oregano.

Note: Use minced (ground) beef instead of the pork and veal, if you prefer.

VEAL AGNOLOTTI WITH ALFREDO SAUCE

SERVES 4–6

625 g (1 lb 6 oz) veal agnolotti

90 g (3¼ oz) butter

150 g (5½ oz/1½ cups) grated parmesan cheese

300 ml (10½ fl oz) pouring cream

2 tablespoons chopped marjoram (see Note)

1 **Cook the pasta** in a large saucepan of boiling salted water until just tender. Drain well and return to the pan to keep warm.

2 **Meanwhile,** melt the butter in a saucepan over low heat. Add the parmesan and cream and bring to the boil. Reduce the heat and simmer, stirring constantly, for 2 minutes, or until the sauce has thickened slightly. Stir in the marjoram and season. Toss the sauce through the pasta.

Note: Any fresh herb such as parsley, thyme, chervil or dill can be used instead of marjoram.

CRESTI DI GALLO WITH CREAMY TOMATO SAUCE

SERVES 4

400 g (14 oz) cresti di gallo (see Note)

1 tablespoon olive oil

175 g (6 oz) bacon, thinly sliced

500 g (1 lb 2 oz) roma (plum) tomatoes, roughly chopped

125 ml (4 fl oz/½ cup) pouring cream

2 tablespoons sun-dried tomato pesto

2 tablespoons finely chopped flat-leaf (Italian) parsley

50 g (1¾ oz/½ cup) finely grated parmesan cheese

1 Cook the pasta in a large saucepan of boiling salted water until just tender. Drain well and return to the pan to keep warm.

2 Meanwhile, heat the oil in a frying pan over high heat. Add the bacon and cook for 2 minutes, or until starting to brown. Reduce the heat to medium. Add the tomato and cook, stirring frequently, for 2 minutes, or until the tomato has softened but still holds its shape.

3 Add the cream and tomato pesto and stir until heated through. Remove from the heat. Add the parsley, then toss the sauce through the pasta with the parmesan.

Note: Cresti di gallo pasta is named after the Italian word for 'cockscombs' because of its similarity to the crest of a rooster. You can also use cotelli or fusilli.

PEPPERED PORK, ZUCCHINI AND GARGANELLI

450 g (1 lb) pork fillet

3–4 teaspoons cracked black peppercorns

80 g (2¾ oz) butter

250 g (9 oz) garganelli

1 onion, halved and thinly sliced

2 large zucchini (courgette), thinly sliced

1 large handful fresh basil, torn

155 g (5½ oz/¾ cup) small black olives

60 g (2¼ oz/½ cup) grated romano cheese

1 Cut the pork fillet in half widthways and roll in the pepper and some salt.

2 Heat half the butter in a large deep frying pan over medium heat. Add the pork and cook for 4 minutes on each side, or until golden brown and just cooked through. Remove from the pan and cut into 5 mm (¼ inch) slices, then set aside and keep warm.

3 Cook the pasta in a large saucepan of boiling salted water until just tender. Drain well and return to the pan to keep warm.

4 Meanwhile, melt the remaining butter in the frying pan over medium heat. Add the onion and cook, stirring, for about 3 minutes, or until soft.

5 Add the zucchini and toss for 5 minutes, or until starting to soften.

6 Add the basil, olives, sliced pork and any juices and toss well. Stir the pork mixture through the pasta, then season. Serve topped with the romano cheese.

PASTITSIO

2 tablespoons oil

4 garlic cloves, crushed

2 onions, chopped

1 kg (2 lb 4 oz) minced (ground) beef

1 kg (2 lb 4 oz) tinned peeled tomatoes, chopped

250 ml (9 fl oz/1 cup) dry red wine

250 ml (9 fl oz/1 cup) beef stock

1 bay leaf

1 teaspoon dried mixed herbs

350 g (12 oz) ziti

3 eggs, lightly beaten

500 g (1 lb 2 oz) Greek-style yoghurt

200 g (7 oz) kefalotyri cheese, grated (see Note)

½ teaspoon ground nutmeg

60 g (2¼ oz/½ cup) grated cheddar cheese

oakleaf lettuce, to serve

1   Heat the oil in a large heavy-based frying pan over medium heat. Cook the garlic and onion for 5 minutes, or until the onion is soft.

2   Add the beef and cook over high heat until browned, then drain off any excess fat.

3   Add the tomato, wine, stock, bay leaf and herbs and bring to the boil. Reduce the heat and simmer for 40 minutes. Season well.

4   Preheat the oven to 180°C (350°F/Gas 4).

5   Meanwhile, cook the pasta in a large saucepan of boiling salted water until just tender. Drain well and spread in the base of a large ovenproof dish. Pour in half the egg and top with the sauce.

6   Combine the yoghurt, remaining egg, kefalotyri and nutmeg and pour over the top. Sprinkle with the cheddar and bake for 40 minutes, or until golden brown. Serve with oakleaf lettuce.

Note: Kefalotyri is a hard Greek sheep's or goat's milk cheese. Parmesan or pecorino cheese can be substituted.

SPAGHETTI BOLOGNESE

SERVES 4

60 g (2¼ oz) butter

1 onion, finely chopped

2 garlic cloves, crushed

1 celery stalk, finely chopped

1 carrot, diced

50 g (1¾ oz) piece pancetta, diced

500 g (1 lb 2 oz) minced (ground) beef

1 tablespoon chopped oregano

250 ml (9 fl oz/1 cup) red wine

500 ml (17 fl oz/2 cups) beef stock

2 tablespoons tomato paste (concentrated purée)

800 g (1 lb 12 oz) tinned chopped tomatoes

400 g (14 oz) spaghetti

3 tablespoons grated parmesan cheese

1 Melt the butter in a large saucepan over medium heat. Add the onion and cook for 2–3 minutes, or until soft.

2 Add the garlic, celery and carrot, and cook, stirring, over low heat, for 5 minutes. Increase the heat to high, add the pancetta, beef and oregano, and cook for 4–5 minutes or until browned.

3 Pour in the wine, reduce the heat and simmer for 4–5 minutes, or until absorbed.

4 Add the stock, tomato paste and tomatoes and season. Cover with a lid and simmer for 1½ hours, stirring occasionally. Uncover and simmer for a further 1 hour, stirring occasionally.

5 Cook the pasta in a large saucepan of boiling salted water until just tender. Drain well and return to the pan to keep warm.

6 Top the pasta with the sauce. Serve with the parmesan.

FETTUCINE WITH CHERRY TOMATOES AND BACON

SERVES 4

4 garlic cloves, unpeeled

80 ml (2½ fl oz/⅓ cup) olive oil

250 g (9 oz) cherry tomatoes

300 g (10½ oz) short cut bacon

350 g (12 oz) fresh fettucine

1 tablespoon white wine vinegar

2 tablespoons roughly chopped fresh basil

2 ripe avocados, diced

1 **Preheat the oven** to 200°C (400°F/Gas 6). Place the garlic at one end of a roasting tin and drizzle with 2 tablespoons of the olive oil. Place the tomatoes at the other end and season well. Bake for 10 minutes, then remove the garlic. Return the tomatoes to the oven for a further 5–10 minutes, or until soft.

2 **Cook the bacon** under a hot grill for 4–5 minutes each side, or until crisp and golden. Roughly chop.

3 **Meanwhile,** cook the pasta in a large pan of boiling salted water until just tender. Drain well and transfer to a large bowl. Drizzle 1 tablespoon of olive oil over the pasta and toss well. Season with salt and pepper. Keep warm.

4 **Slit the skin** of each garlic clove and squeeze the garlic out. Place in a screw-top jar with the vinegar, chopped basil and remaining oil and shake well to combine.

5 **Add the tomatoes** and their juices, bacon and avocado to the fettucine, pour on the dressing and toss well. Garnish with a few whole fresh basil leaves and serve with crusty bread.

CREAMY GNOCCHI WITH PEAS AND PROSCIUTTO

SERVES 4

100 g (3½ oz) thinly sliced prosciutto
3 teaspoons oil
2 eggs
250 ml (9 fl oz/1 cup) cream
35 g (1¼ oz/⅓ cup) finely grated parmesan cheese
2 tablespoons chopped fresh flat-leaf (Italian) parsley
1 tablespoon snipped fresh chives
250 g (9 oz) fresh or frozen peas
500 g (1 lb 2 oz) pasta shells or gnocchi

1 Cut the prosciutto into thin strips. Heat the oil in a frying pan over medium heat, add the prosciutto and cook for 2 minutes, or until crisp. Drain on paper towels.

2 Whisk together the eggs, cream, parmesan and herbs in a large bowl.

3 Bring a large saucepan of salted water to the boil. Add the peas and cook for 5 minutes, or until just tender. Leaving the pan on the heat, use a slotted spoon and transfer the peas to the bowl of cream mixture, and then add 3 tablespoons of the cooking liquid to the same bowl. Using a potato masher or the back of a fork, roughly mash the peas.

4 Add the pasta to the boiling water and cook until just tender. Drain well, then return to the pan.

5 Add the cream mixture, then warm through over low heat, gently stirring for about 30 seconds until the gnocchi is coated in the sauce. Season to taste with salt and cracked black pepper.

6 Divide among warmed plates, top with the prosciutto and serve immediately.

Note: Be careful not to overheat or cook for too long or the egg will begin to set to scrambled egg.

PENNE WITH PUMPKIN, RICOTTA AND PROSCIUTTO

SERVES 4

500 g (1 lb 2 oz) penne

460 g (1 lb) butternut pumpkin, cut into small cubes

60 ml (2 fl oz/¼ cup) extra virgin olive oil

2 garlic cloves, crushed

100 g (3½ oz) semi-dried tomatoes (sun-blushed), chopped

4 slices prosciutto, chopped

250 g (9 oz) baked ricotta, cut into small cubes

3 tablespoons shredded fresh basil

1 Cook the pasta in a large pan of rapidly boiling salted water until just tender. Drain well.

2 Meanwhile, cook the pumpkin in a saucepan of boiling water for 10–12 minutes, or until just tender, then drain.

3 Heat the oil in a large saucepan, add the garlic and cook over medium heat for 30 seconds. Add the tomato, prosciutto, pumpkin and penne and toss gently over low heat for 1–2 minutes, or until heated through.

4 Add the baked ricotta and the basil, season with salt and cracked black pepper and serve immediately.

BUCATINI WITH SAUSAGE AND FENNEL SEED

SERVES 4

500 g (1 lb 2 oz) good-quality Italian sausages
2 tablespoons olive oil
3 garlic cloves, chopped
1 teaspoon fennel seeds
½ teaspoon chilli flakes
2 x 425 g (14 oz) tins chopped tomatoes
500 g (1 lb 2 oz) bucatini
1 teaspoon balsamic vinegar
1 small handful fresh basil, chopped

1 **Heat a frying pan** over high heat, add the sausages and cook, turning, for 8–10 minutes, or until well browned and cooked through. Remove, cool slightly and slice thinly on the diagonal.

2 **Heat the oil** in a saucepan, add the garlic and cook over medium heat for 1 minute. Add the fennel seeds and chilli flakes and cook for a further minute. Stir in the tomato and bring to the boil, then reduce the heat and simmer, covered, for 20 minutes.

3 **Meanwhile,** cook the pasta in a large pan of rapidly boiling salted water until just tender. Drain and return to the pan to keep warm.

4 **Add the sausages** to the sauce and cook, uncovered, for 5 minutes to heat through.

5 **Stir in the balsamic vinegar** and basil. Divide the pasta among four bowls, top with the sauce and serve.

PROSCIUTTO AND SWEET POTATO PENNE

SERVES 4

500 g (1 lb 2 oz) penne

500 g (1 lb 2 oz) orange sweet potato, diced

2 tablespoons extra virgin olive oil

5 spring onions (scallions), sliced

2 small garlic cloves, crushed

8 thin slices prosciutto, chopped

125 g (4½ oz) sun-dried tomatoes in oil, drained and sliced

2 small handfuls shredded fresh basil leaves

1 Cook the penne in a large pan of rapidly boiling salted water until al dente. Drain well and return to the pan to keep warm.

2 Meanwhile, steam the sweet potato for 5 minutes, or until tender.

3 Heat the oil in a saucepan, add the spring onion, garlic and sweet potato and stir over medium heat for 2–3 minutes, or until the spring onion is soft. Add the prosciutto and tomato and cook for a further 1 minute.

4 Add the sweet potato mixture to the penne and toss over low heat until heated through. Add the basil and season with black pepper.

5 Serve immediately with crusty bread.

Note: Orange sweet potato is also known as kumera.

PASTA SHELLS WITH SAUSAGE AND TOMATO

SERVES 4

500 g (1 lb 2 oz) pasta shells or gnocchi
2 tablespoons olive oil
400 g (14 oz) thin Italian sausages
1 red onion, finely chopped
2 garlic cloves, finely chopped
2 x 415 g (14 oz) tins chopped tomatoes
1 teaspoon caster (superfine) sugar
2 large handfuls fresh basil, torn
45 g (1¾ oz/½ cup) grated pecorino cheese

1 **Cook the pasta** in a large pan of rapidly boiling salted water until just tender. Drain. Return to pan to keep warm.

2 **Meanwhile,** heat 2 teaspoons of the oil in a large frying pan. Add the sausages and cook, turning, for 5 minutes, or until well browned and cooked through. Drain on paper towels, then slice when cooled enough to hold. Keep warm.

3 **Wipe clean the frying pan** and heat the remaining oil. Add the onion and garlic and cook over medium heat for 2 minutes, or until the onion has softened.

4 **Add the tomato,** sugar and 250 ml (8 fl oz/1 cup) water and season well. Reduce the heat and simmer for about 12 minutes, or until thickened and reduced a little.

5 **Pour the sauce** over the pasta and stir through the sausage, basil and half the cheese. Serve hot, sprinkled with the remaining cheese.

SPAGHETTI WITH MEATBALLS

SERVES 4

MEATBALLS

500 g (1 lb 2 oz) minced (ground) beef

40 g (1½ oz) fresh breadcrumbs

1 onion, finely chopped

2 garlic cloves, crushed

2 teaspoons Worcestershire sauce

1 teaspoon dried oregano

30 g (1 oz/¼ cup) plain (all-purpose) flour

2 tablespoons olive oil

SAUCE

800 g (1 lb 12 oz) tinned chopped tomatoes

1 tablespoon olive oil

1 onion, finely chopped

2 garlic cloves, crushed

2 tablespoons tomato paste (concentrated purée)

120 ml (4 fl oz) beef stock

2 teaspoons sugar

500 g (1 lb 2 oz) spaghetti

grated parmesan cheese, to serve

1 **Combine the beef,** breadcrumbs, onion, garlic, Worcestershire sauce and oregano in a bowl and season. Mix well. Roll level tablespoons of the mixture into balls, dust with the flour and shake off the excess. Heat the oil in a frying pan over high heat. Cook the meatballs in batches, turning, until browned all over. Drain well.

2 **Purée the tomatoes** in a food processor.

3 **Heat the oil** in a frying pan over medium heat. Add the onion and cook until soft. Add the garlic and cook for 1 minute.

4 **Add the puréed tomatoes,** tomato paste, stock and sugar and stir to combine. Bring to the boil and add the meatballs. Reduce the heat and simmer for 15 minutes. Season.

5 **Meanwhile,** cook the pasta in a large saucepan of boiling salted water until just tender. Drain well and return to the pan to keep warm.

6 **Top the pasta** with the meatballs and sauce. Serve with parmesan.

TAGLIATELLE WITH BEEF RAGÙ

SERVES 4

100 g (3½ oz) streaky bacon or pancetta (not trimmed), finely chopped
1 onion, finely chopped
3 garlic cloves, crushed
1 bay leaf
800 g (1 lb 12 oz) lean minced (ground) beef
500 ml (17 fl oz/2 cups) red wine
90 g (3¼ oz/⅓ cup) tomato paste (concentrated purée)
400 g (14 oz) tagliatelle
freshly grated parmesan cheese, to serve

1 Heat a large deep frying pan over medium–high heat. Add the bacon or pancetta and cook for 2 minutes, or until soft and just starting to brown.

2 Add the onion, garlic and bay leaf and cook for 2 minutes, or until the onion is soft and just starting to brown.

3 Add the beef and stir for about 4 minutes or until the beef browns, breaking up any lumps with the back of a wooden spoon.

4 Add the wine, tomato paste and 250 ml (9 fl oz/1 cup) water and stir well. Bring to the boil, then reduce the heat and simmer, covered, for 40 minutes. Remove the lid and cook for a further 40 minutes, or until reduced to a thick sauce.

5 Meanwhile, cook the pasta in a large saucepan of boiling salted water until just tender. Drain well and return to the pan to keep warm.

6 Serve the sauce over the pasta and top with grated parmesan.

BAKED SHELLS WITH RICOTTA AND PROSCIUTTO

SERVES 4

24 conchiglione (large pasta shells)

200 g (7 oz) prosciutto, roughly chopped

2 tablespoons snipped chives

3 large handfuls chopped fresh basil

90 g (3¼ oz) butter

500 g (1 lb 2 oz) ricotta cheese

150 g (5 oz/1 cup) chopped sun-dried capsicum (peppers)

100 g (3½ oz/1 cup) grated parmesan cheese

750 g (1 lb 10 oz/3 cups) bottled tomato pasta sauce

1 **Preheat the oven** to 180°C (350°F/Gas 4).

2 **Cook the pasta** in a large pan of rapidly boiling salted water until al dente. Drain well and return to the pan to keep warm.

3 **Place the prosciutto,** chives and basil in a food processor or blender and pulse until chopped.

4 **Melt the butter** in a large frying pan over medium heat. Add the prosciutto mixture and cook for about 5 minutes, or until the prosciutto is golden and crisp.

5 **Transfer the mixture** to a bowl, add the ricotta, capsicum and a quarter of the parmesan. Stir well and season to taste.

6 **Pour the pasta sauce** into a 3 litre (105 fl oz/12 cups) ovenproof dish. Spoon the ricotta mixture into the pasta shells and place in the dish. Sprinkle the remaining parmesan over the shells and bake for 25–30 minutes, or until golden. Spoon the sauce over the shells and serve.

HAM AND CHEESE PASTA BAKE

SERVES 4

1½ tablespoons olive oil

1 onion, finely chopped

300 g (10½ oz) leg ham, sliced 3 mm (⅛ inch) thick and cut into 5 cm (2 inch) lengths

600 ml (21 fl oz) pouring cream

300 g (10½ oz) cooked fresh peas or frozen peas, thawed

375 g (13 oz) conchiglione

3 tablespoons roughly chopped basil

250 g (9 oz) grated mature cheddar cheese

1   Preheat the oven to 200°C (400°F/Gas 6). Lightly grease a 2.5 litre (87 fl oz/10 cup) ovenproof ceramic dish.

2   Heat 1 tablespoon of the oil in a frying pan over medium heat. Cook the onion, stirring frequently, for 5 minutes or until soft.

3   Add the remaining oil, then the ham and cook, stirring, for 1 minute. Pour the cream into the pan, bring to the boil, then reduce the heat and simmer for 6 minutes.

4   Add the peas and cook for a further 2–4 minutes, or until the mixture has thickened slightly. Season.

5   Meanwhile, cook the pasta in a large saucepan of boiling salted water until just tender. Drain well and return to the pan to keep warm.

6   Add the sauce to the pasta, then stir in the basil and three-quarters of the cheese. Season.

7   Add the mixture to the prepared dish, sprinkle on the remaining cheese and bake for 20 minutes, or until the top is golden brown.

TORTELLINI WITH SPECK, ASPARAGUS AND TOMATO

SERVES 4–6

200 g (7 oz) piece speck or bacon (skin removed), roughly chopped

4 tomatoes

310 g (11 oz) asparagus, cut into 3 cm (1¼ inch) lengths

500 g (1 lb 2 oz) cheese tortellini

1 tablespoon olive oil

1 red onion, thinly sliced

1 tablespoon tomato paste (concentrated purée)

125 ml (4 fl oz/½ cup) chicken stock

2 teaspoons thyme leaves

1 Put the speck in a food processor and pulse until chopped.

2 Score a cross in the base of the tomatoes. Put in a heatproof bowl and cover with boiling water. Leave for 30 seconds, then transfer to cold water and peel the skin away from the cross. Roughly chop.

3 Cook the asparagus in a large saucepan of boiling water for 2 minutes, or until just tender. Remove with a slotted spoon and refresh in cold water. Drain.

4 Cook the pasta in the same boiling water and cook until just tender . Drain well and return to the pan to keep warm.

5 Meanwhile, heat the oil in a saucepan over medium heat. Add the speck and onion and cook, stirring, for 2–3 minutes, or until the onion is soft.

6 Add the tomato, tomato paste, stock and thyme and season. Cook, stirring, for 5 minutes.

7 Add the pasta and asparagus to the tomato mixture and stir over low heat until warmed through.

PASTA AMATRICIANA

SERVES 4–6

2 tablespoons olive oil

200 g (7 oz) pancetta, thinly sliced

1 red onion, finely chopped

2 garlic cloves, finely chopped

1 teaspoon chilli flakes

2 teaspoons finely chopped rosemary

2 x 400 g (14 oz) tins chopped tomatoes

500 g (1 lb 2 oz) bucatini or spaghetti

1 large handful chopped flat-leaf (Italian) parsley

1 Heat the oil in a frying pan and cook the pancetta over medium heat for 6–8 minutes, or until crisp.

2 Add the onion, garlic, chilli flakes and chopped rosemary and cook for 4–5 minutes more, or until the onion has softened.

3 Add the tomato to the pan, season with salt and pepper, and bring to the boil. Reduce the heat to low and simmer for 20 minutes, or until the sauce is reduced and very thick.

4 Meanwhile, cook the pasta in a large saucepan of boiling salted water until just tender.

5 Toss the sauce with the hot pasta and parsley and serve.

RICH BEEF AND MUSHROOM LASAGNE

SERVES 4

1 tablespoon olive oil

2 garlic cloves, crushed

1 onion, chopped

1 carrot, grated

1 celery stalk, diced

125 g (4½ oz) mushrooms, chopped

600 g (1 lb 5 oz) minced ground beef

600 ml (21 fl oz/2½ cups) Italian tomato
    passata

1 teaspoon dried oregano leaves

300 g (10½ oz) instant lasagne sheets

100 g (3½ oz/1 cup) grated parmesan
    cheese

CHEESE SAUCE

60 g (2¼ oz) butter

40 g (1½ oz/⅓ cup) plain (all-purpose)
    flour

1 litre (35 fl oz/4 cups) milk

½ teaspoon ground nutmeg

125 g (4½ oz/1 cup) grated cheddar
    cheese

1 Heat the oil in a large heavy-based pan. Add the garlic, onion, carrot, celery and mushroom. Cook, stirring, over medium heat for 2–3 minutes, or until the onion has softened.

2 Increase the heat, add the mince and stir for a further 3–4 minutes, or until the mince has browned and is well broken up.

3 Add the tomato passata, oregano and 500 ml (16 fl oz/ 2 cups) water. Bring to the boil, stirring, then lower the heat and simmer for 1 hour, or until the mixture has thickened. Stir occasionally.

4 To make the cheese sauce, melt the butter in a heavy-based pan. Add the flour and cook, stirring, for 1 minute until pale and foaming. Remove from the heat, gradually add the milk and stir until smooth. Return to the heat and stir continuously for 3–4 minutes, or until the sauce boils and thickens. Cook over low heat for 1 minute. Stir in the nutmeg and Cheddar. Season.

5 To assemble, preheat the oven to 180°C (350°F/Gas 4). Grease a 2.5 litre (87 fl oz/10 cup) baking dish. Arrange four lasagne sheets over the base of the baking dish. Spread one-third of the meat mixture over the sheets, then pour over about 185 ml (6 fl oz/¾ cup) of the cheese sauce. Repeat with two more layers of each. Top with the four remaining lasagne sheets, then with the remaining sauce and finish with the parmesan. Bake for 45 minutes, or until golden. Leave to stand for 5 minutes before serving.

GOULASH WITH FUSILLI

SERVES 4

400 g (14 oz) fusilli

2 tablespoons olive oil

1 large onion, sliced into thin wedges

600 g (1 lb 5 oz) rump steak, trimmed and cut into 2 cm (¾ inch) cubes

1 tablespoon plain (all-purpose) flour

1 small green capsicum (pepper), diced

850 g (1 lb 14 oz) tinned diced tomatoes

1 teaspoon hot paprika

80 g (2¾ oz/⅓ cup) light sour cream

1 Cook the pasta in a large saucepan of boiling salted water until just tender. Drain well and return to the pan to keep warm.

2 Meanwhile, heat 1 tablespoon of the olive oil in a large frying pan over medium heat. Add the onion and cook, stirring, for 4–5 minutes, or until softened and golden. Remove the onion from the pan.

3 Heat the remaining olive oil in the same frying pan over high heat. Toss the steak cubes in the flour, shaking off any excess, then add to the pan and cook for 2 minutes to brown on all sides. Add the capsicum, tomato, paprika and the cooked onion and stir to combine.

4 Bring the mixture to the boil, then reduce the heat and simmer for 8–10 minutes, stirring occasionally. Season.

5 To serve, spoon the goulash mixture over the pasta and top with sour cream.

PAPPARDELLE WITH SALAMI, LEEK AND PROVOLONE CHEESE

SERVES 4

375 g (13 oz) pappardelle

2 tablespoons olive oil

2 leeks, thinly sliced (including some of the green section)

2 tablespoons white wine

2 x 400 g (14 oz) tins chopped tomatoes

150 g (6 oz) sliced mild salami, cut into strips

1 small handful fresh basil leaves, torn

125 g (4½ oz) provolone cheese, sliced into strips

30 g (1 oz) grated parmesan cheese

1 Cook the pasta in a large pan of rapidly boiling salted water until just tender. Drain and return to the pan to keep warm.

2 Meanwhile, heat the olive oil in a large deep frying pan, add the leek and cook over low heat for 4 minutes, or until soft but not browned. Increase the heat to medium, add the wine and stir until almost evaporated.

3 Add the tomato and salami, season with salt and cracked black pepper and simmer for 5 minutes, or until reduced slightly.

4 Toss the tomato sauce mixture, basil and provolone lightly through the pasta. Sprinkle with parmesan and serve.

VEAL TORTELLINI WITH PUMPKIN AND BASIL BUTTER

SERVES 4–6

1 kg (2 lb 4 oz) jap pumpkin
    (winter squash), cut into 2 cm
    (¾ inch) cubes

600 g (1 lb 5 oz) veal tortellini

100 g (3½ oz) butter

3 garlic cloves, crushed

80 g (2¾ oz/½ cup) pine nuts

2 large handfuls shredded basil

200 g (7 oz/1⅓ cups) feta cheese,
    crumbled

1 Preheat the oven to 220°C (425°F/Gas 7). Line a baking tray with baking paper. Place the pumpkin on the prepared tray and season well. Bake for 30 minutes, or until tender.

2 Meanwhile, cook the pasta in a large saucepan of boiling salted water until just tender. Drain well and return to the pan to keep warm.

3 Heat the butter in a small frying pan over medium heat until foaming. Add the garlic and pine nuts and cook for 3–5 minutes, or until the nuts are starting to turn golden. Remove from the heat and add the basil. Toss the basil butter, pumpkin and feta through the pasta.

AGNOLOTTI WITH CREAMY SEMI-DRIED TOMATO SAUCE

SERVES 4

4 bacon slices

625 g (1 lb 6 oz) veal or chicken agnolotti

1 tablespoon olive oil

2 garlic cloves, finely chopped

110 g (3¾ oz/⅔ cup) thinly sliced semi-dried (sun-blushed) tomatoes

1 tablespoon chopped thyme

375 ml (13 fl oz/1½ cups) pouring cream

1 teaspoon finely grated lemon zest

35 g (1¼ oz/⅓ cup) finely grated parmesan cheese

1 Grill (broil) the bacon for 5 minutes on each side, or until crisp and golden. Remove, drain well on paper towel, then break into pieces.

2 Cook the pasta in a large saucepan of boiling salted water until just tender. Drain well and return to the pan to keep warm.

3 Heat the oil in a frying pan over medium heat. Cook the garlic for 1 minute, or until just golden. Add the tomato and thyme and cook for a further 1 minute.

4 Add the cream, bring to the boil, then reduce the heat and simmer for about 6–8 minutes, or until the cream has thickened and reduced by one-third. Season and add the lemon zest and 2 tablespoons of the parmesan.

5 Pour the sauce over the pasta. Sprinkle with the remaining parmesan and the bacon pieces.

BAKED BEEF WITH VERMICELLI CAKE

SERVES 4

85 g (3 oz) butter

1 onion, chopped

500 g (1 lb 2 oz) minced (ground) beef

800 g (1 lb 12 oz) bottled tomato pasta sauce

2 tablespoons tomato paste (concentrated purée)

250 g (9 oz) vermicelli or spaghettini

30 g (1 oz/¼ cup) plain (all-purpose) flour

375 ml (13 fl oz/1¼ cups) milk

155 g (5½ oz/1¼ cups) grated cheddar cheese

1 **Preheat the oven** to 180°C (350°F/Gas 4). Grease a 24 cm (9 inch) round deep springform tin.

2 **Melt 20 g** (¾ oz) of the butter in a large deep frying pan and cook the onion over medium heat for 2–3 minutes, or until soft.

3 **Add the mince,** breaking up any lumps with the back of a spoon, and cook for 4–5 minutes, or until browned.

4 **Stir in the pasta sauce** and tomato paste, reduce the heat and simmer for 20–25 minutes. Season.

5 **Cook the pasta** in a large saucepan of boiling salted water until just tender. Drain and rinse.

6 **Meanwhile,** melt the remaining butter in a saucepan over low heat. Stir in the flour and cook for 1 minute, or until pale and foaming. Remove from the heat and gradually stir in the milk. Return to the heat and stir constantly until the sauce boils and thickens. Reduce the heat and simmer for 2 minutes.

7 **Spread half the pasta** over the base of the tin, then cover with half the meat sauce. Cover with the remaining pasta, pressing it down. Spoon on the remaining meat sauce and then pour on the white sauce. Sprinkle with cheese and cook for 15 minutes. Stand for 10 minutes before removing from the tin. Cut into wedges.

SEAFOOD

CRAB, CAMEMBERT AND FUSILLI FRITTATA

SERVES 4–6

90 g (3 oz) fusilli

1 tablespoon olive oil

1 very small red onion, finely chopped

1 large roma (plum) tomato, roughly chopped

60 g (1/3 cup/2 oz) semi-dried tomatoes, roughly chopped

2 tablespoons finely chopped fresh coriander leaves

150 g (5 oz/2/3 cup) cooked fresh or canned crabmeat

150 g (5 oz) camembert, rind removed, cut into small pieces

6 eggs plus 2 egg yolks

1 **Cook the pasta** in a large pan of rapidly boiling salted water until just tender. Drain and set aside to cool a little.

2 **Meanwhile,** heat half the oil in a small frying pan over low heat, add the onion and cook for 4–5 minutes, or until softened but not browned. Transfer to a bowl and add the Roma tomato, semi-dried tomatoes and coriander.

3 **Squeeze out any excess moisture** from the crab meat and add to the bowl. Add half the cheese and the cooled pasta. Mix well.

4 **Beat together** the six eggs and the two extra yolks, then stir into the frittata mixture. Season with salt and pepper.

5 **Heat the remaining oil** in the frying pan, pour in the frittata mixture and cook over low heat for 25 minutes.

6 **Preheat the grill** to low. Scatter remaining camembert over the frittata before placing it under the grill for about 12 minutes, or until cooked and golden brown on top. Remove from the grill and leave for 5 minutes. Cut into slices and serve immediately.

SPAGHETTINI WITH ANCHOVIES, CAPERS AND CHILLI

SERVES 4

400 g (14 oz) spaghettini

125 ml (4 fl oz/½ cup) olive oil

4 garlic cloves, finely chopped

10 anchovy fillets, chopped

1 tablespoon baby capers, rinsed and squeezed dry

1 teaspoon chilli flakes

2 tablespoons lemon juice

2 teaspoons finely grated lemon zest

3 tablespoons chopped flat-leaf (Italian) parsley

3 tablespoons chopped basil leaves

3 tablespoons chopped mint

50 g (1¾ oz/½ cup) coarsely grated parmesan cheese, plus extra, to serve

extra virgin olive oil, to drizzle

1 **Cook the pasta** in a large saucepan of boiling salted water until just tender. Drain well and return to the pan to keep warm.

2 **Heat the oil** in a frying pan over medium heat. Cook the garlic for 2–3 minutes, or until starting to brown. Add the anchovies, capers and chilli and cook for 1 minute.

3 **Add the pasta** to the pan with the lemon juice, zest, parsley, basil, mint and parmesan. Season and toss together.

4 **To serve,** drizzle with a little extra oil and sprinkle with the parmesan.

SPAGHETTI VONGOLE

SERVES 4

1 kg (2 lb 4 oz) baby clams (vongole)

375 g (13 oz) spaghetti

125 ml (4 fl oz/½ cup) extra virgin olive oil

40 g (1½ oz) butter

1 small onion, very finely chopped

6 large garlic cloves, finely chopped

125 ml (4 fl oz/½ cup) dry white wine

1 small red chilli, seeded and finely chopped

15 g (½ oz) chopped flat-leaf (Italian) parsley

1   Scrub the clams with a small stiff brush to remove any grit, discarding any that are open or cracked. Soak and rinse the clams in several changes of water over 1 hour, or until the water is clean and free of grit. Drain and set aside.

2   Cook the pasta in a large saucepan of boiling salted water until just tender. Drain well and return to the pan to keep warm.

3   Heat the oil and 1 tablespoon of the butter in a large saucepan over medium heat. Add the onion and half the garlic and cook for 10 minutes, or until lightly golden.

4   Add the wine and cook for 2 minutes. Add the clams, chilli and the remaining butter and garlic. Cook, covered, for 8 minutes, shaking regularly, until the clams pop open. Discard any that are still closed.

5   Stir in the parsley and season. Add the pasta and toss together.

CREAMY TOMATO AND PRAWN TAGLIATELLE

SERVES 4

400 g (14 oz) dried egg tagliatelle

1 tablespoon olive oil

3 garlic cloves, finely chopped

20 medium raw prawns (shrimp), peeled and deveined, with tails intact

550 g (1 lb 4 oz) roma (plum) tomatoes, diced

2 tablespoons thinly sliced basil

125 ml (4 fl oz/½ cup) white wine

4 tablespoons pouring cream

basil leaves, to garnish

1 Cook the pasta in a large saucepan of boiling salted water until just tender. Drain well, reserving 2 tablespoons of the cooking water. Return the pasta to the pan to keep warm.

2 Heat the oil and garlic in a large frying pan over low heat for 1–2 minutes. Increase the heat to medium, add the prawns and cook for 3–5 minutes, stirring frequently until cooked. Remove the prawns and keep warm.

3 Add the tomato and sliced basil and stir for 3 minutes, or until the tomato is soft. Pour in the wine and cream, bring to the boil and simmer for 2 minutes.

4 Purée the sauce in a blender. Return to the pan, then add the reserved pasta water and bring to a simmer.

5 Stir in the prawns until heated through. Toss through the pasta and serve garnished with the basil leaves.

SPAGHETTINI WITH SQUID IN BLACK INK

SERVES 4

1 kg (2 lb 4 oz) squid

2 tablespoons olive oil

1 onion, finely chopped

6 garlic cloves, finely chopped

1 bay leaf

1 small red chilli, seeded and thinly sliced

4 tablespoons white wine

4 tablespoons dry vermouth

250 ml (9 fl oz/1 cup) fish stock

60 g (2¼ oz/¼ cup) tomato paste (concentrated purée)

500 ml (17 fl oz/2 cups) tomato passata (puréed tomatoes)

15 g (½ oz) squid ink

500 g (1 lb 2 oz) spaghettini

½ teaspoon Pernod, or other aniseed-flavoured liqueur (optional)

4 tablespoons chopped flat-leaf (Italian) parsley

1 garlic clove, extra, crushed

1 **To clean the squid,** gently pull the tentacles away from the tube. Remove the intestines from the tentacles by cutting under the eyes, then remove the beak if it remains in the centre of the tentacles by using your fingers to push up the centre. Pull away the quill from inside the body and remove. Remove and discard any white membrane. Pull away the skin from the hood. Slice the squid into rings.

2 **Heat the oil** in a saucepan over medium heat. Add the onion and cook until golden.

3 **Add the garlic,** bay leaf and chilli and cook for 2 minutes. Stir in the wine, vermouth, stock, tomato paste, passata and 250 ml (9 fl oz/1 cup) water. Increase the heat to high and bring to the boil. Reduce to a simmer. Cook for 45 minutes, or until the liquid has reduced by half.

4 **Add the squid ink** and cook for 2 minutes.

5 **Meanwhile,** cook the pasta in a large saucepan of boiling salted water until just tender. Drain and return to the pan.

6 **Add the squid rings** and Pernod. Cook for 4 minutes, or until cooked through. Stir in the parsley and the extra garlic and season.

SUMMER SEAFOOD MARINARA

SERVES 4

300 g (10 oz) fresh saffron angel hair pasta

1 tablespoon extra virgin olive oil

30 g (1 oz) butter

2 garlic cloves, finely chopped

1 large onion, finely chopped

1 small red chilli, finely chopped

600 g (1 lb 5 oz) tinned peeled tomatoes, chopped

250 ml (9 fl oz/1 cup) white wine

zest of 1 lemon

½ tablespoon sugar

200 g (7 oz) scallops without roe

500 g (1 lb 2 oz) raw prawns (shrimp), peeled and deveined

300 g (10½ oz) clams (vongole)

1 Cook the pasta in a large saucepan of boiling salted water until just tender. Drain well and return to the pan to keep warm.

2 Heat the oil and butter in a large frying pan over medium heat. Add the garlic, onion and chilli and cook for 5 minutes, or until soft.

3 Add the tomatoes and wine and bring to the boil. Cook for 10 minutes, or until the sauce has reduced and thickened slightly.

4 Add the lemon zest, sugar, scallops, prawns and clams. Cook, covered, for 5 minutes, or until the seafood is tender. Discard any clams that do not open. Season and serve the pasta topped with the sauce.

FUSILLI WITH TUNA, CAPERS AND PARSLEY

SERVES 4

425 g (15 oz) tinned tuna in springwater, drained

2 tablespoons olive oil

2 garlic cloves, finely chopped

2 small red chillies, finely chopped

3 tablespoons capers, rinsed and squeezed dry

1 large handful chopped flat-leaf (Italian) parsley

3 tablespoons lemon juice

375 g (13 oz) fusilli

125 ml (4 fl oz/½ cup) chicken stock

1 **Put the tuna** in a bowl and flake lightly with a fork. Combine the oil, garlic, chilli, capers, parsley and lemon juice in a small bowl. Pour the mixture over the tuna and mix. Season.

2 **Meanwhile,** cook the pasta in a large saucepan of boiling salted water until just tender. Drain well and return to the pan to keep warm.

3 **Toss the tuna mixture** through the pasta, adding enough of the hot chicken stock to make it moist.

SPAGHETTI MARINARA

SERVES 4

TOMATO SAUCE
2 tablespoons olive oil

1 onion, finely chopped

1 carrot, finely chopped

2 garlic cloves, crushed

400 g (14 oz) tinned chopped tomatoes

125 ml (4 fl oz/½ cup) white wine

1 teaspoon sugar

3 tablespoons white wine

3 tablespoons fish stock

1 garlic clove, crushed

12 black mussels, cleaned

375 g (13 oz) spaghetti

30 g (1 oz) butter

125 g (4½ oz) squid, cleaned and cut into rings

125 g (4½ oz) skinless cod fillet, cut into bite-sized pieces

200 g (7 oz) prawns (shrimp), peeled and deveined

1 handful flat-leaf (Italian) parsley, chopped

200 g (7 oz) tinned clams, drained

1 **Heat the oil** in a saucepan over medium heat. Cook the onion and carrot for 10 minutes, or until browned.

2 **Add the garlic,** tomato, wine and sugar. Bring to the boil, then reduce the heat and simmer for 30 minutes, stirring occasionally.

3 **Heat the wine,** stock and garlic in a large saucepan over high heat. Add the mussels. Cover and shake the pan for 5 minutes. Discard any unopened mussels and reserve the cooking liquid.

4 **Cook the pasta** in a large saucepan of boiling salted water until just tender . Drain well and return to the pan to keep warm.

5 **Melt the butter** in a frying pan over medium heat. Stir-fry the squid, cod and prawns in batches for about 2 minutes, or until just cooked.

6 **Add to the tomato sauce** along with the reserved cooking liquid, mussels, parsley and clams. Toss together.

PAPPARDELLE WITH SALMON AND GREMOLATA

SERVES 4

GREMOLATA

2 very large handfuls chopped flat-leaf (Italian) parsley

3 teaspoons grated lemon zest

2 garlic cloves, finely chopped

400 g (14 oz) pappardelle

3 tablespoons extra virgin olive oil

500 g (1 lb 2 oz) fresh salmon fillet

2 teaspoons olive oil, extra

1 To make the gremolata, put the parsley, lemon zest and garlic in a bowl and mix together well.

2 Cook the pasta in a large saucepan of boiling salted water until just tender. Drain well and return to the pan.

3 Add the olive oil and toss gently. Add the gremolata to the pan with the pasta and toss.

4 Remove the skin and any bones from the salmon. Heat the extra olive oil in a frying pan over medium heat. Cook the salmon for 3–4 minutes, turning once during cooking. Take care not to overcook the fish. Flake the salmon into large pieces and toss through the pasta. Season.

SEAFOOD LASAGNE

SERVES 4

1 tablespoon olive oil

30 g (1 oz) butter

1 onion, finely chopped

2 garlic cloves, crushed

400 g (14 oz) prawns (shrimp), peeled and deveined

500 g (1 lb 2 oz) firm white fish fillets, cut into small pieces

250 g (9 oz) scallops with roe

750 g (1 lb 10 oz) ready-made tomato pasta sauce

1 tablespoon tomato paste (concentrated purée)

1 teaspoon soft brown sugar

60 g (2¼ oz/½ cup) grated cheddar cheese

25 g (1 oz/¼ cup) grated parmesan cheese

250 g (9 oz) lasagne sheets

CHEESE SAUCE

120 g (4¼ oz) butter

85 g (3 oz/⅔ cup) plain (all-purpose) flour

1.5 litres (52 fl oz/6 cups) milk

250 g (9 oz/2 cups) grated cheddar cheese

100 g (3½ oz/1 cup) grated parmesan cheese

1 **Preheat the oven** to 180°C (350°F/Gas 4). Grease a 2.5 litre (87 fl oz/10 cup) ovenproof dish.

2 **Heat the oil** and butter in a saucepan. Add the onion and cook for 2–3 minutes. Add the garlic and cook for 30 seconds.

3 **Add the prawns** and fish and cook for 2 minutes, then add the scallops. Cook for 1 minute. Stir in the pasta sauce, tomato paste and sugar and simmer for 5 minutes.

4 **To make the sauce,** melt the butter in a saucepan over low heat, then stir in the flour and cook for 1 minute. Stir in the milk. Simmer for 2 minutes, stirring, then mix in the cheddar and parmesan cheeses. Season.

5 **Line the dish** with a layer of lasagne sheets. Spoon one-third of the seafood sauce into the dish. Top with one-third of the cheese sauce. Repeat until you have three layers, ending with a layer of cheese sauce. Sprinkle with the cheeses. Bake for 30 minutes, or until golden.

WARM PASTA AND SMOKED SALMON STACK

SERVES 4

1.5 kg (3 lb 5 oz) vine-ripened tomatoes

2 garlic cloves, crushed

1 teaspoon sugar

80 ml (2½ fl oz/⅓ cup) olive oil

3 tablespoons chopped fresh flat-leaf (Italian) parsley

6 fresh lasagne sheets

400 g (14 oz) smoked salmon

100 g (3½ oz) baby rocket (arugula) leaves

extra virgin olive oil, for drizzling

1 Score a cross in the base of each tomato and place in a bowl of boiling water for 1 minute. Plunge into cold water and peel the skin away from the cross. Remove the core, then transfer to a food processor or blender and, using the pulse button, process until roughly chopped. Transfer to a saucepan with the garlic and sugar, bring to the boil, then reduce the heat and simmer for 5 minutes, or until reduced slightly. Remove from the heat and gradually whisk in the oil. Stir in the parsley and season. Keep warm.

2 Cut the lasagne sheets in half widthways to give 12 pieces, each about 12 cm (5 inches) squares. Cook the pasta in a large saucepan of boiling water in two batches until just tender. Remove from the water and lay out flat to prevent sticking.

3 Place a pasta sheet on each of four plates. Set aside ⅓ cup of the tomato mix. Spoon half the remaining tomato mixture over the pasta sheets, then half the smoked salmon and rocket leaves. Repeat to give two layers. Finish with a third sheet of pasta.

4 Top each pasta stack with a tablespoon of the tomato sauce, drizzle with a little extra virgin olive oil and serve immediately.

SPAGHETTI WITH SMOKED TUNA AND OLIVES

SERVES 4

800 g (1 lb 12 oz) vine-ripened
   tomatoes

375 g (13 oz) spaghetti

3 x 125 g (4½ oz) tins smoked tuna
   slices in oil

1 red onion, chopped

2 garlic cloves, crushed

1 teaspoon sugar

150 g (5½ oz/1 cup) black olives

2 tablespoons chopped fresh basil

75 g (2½ oz/½ cup) feta cheese,
   crumbled

1 Score a cross in the base of each tomato. Place the tomatoes in a bowl of boiling water for 1 minute, then plunge into cold water and peel the skin away from the cross. Cut in half and remove the seeds with a teaspoon. Roughly chop the flesh.

2 Cook the pasta in a large pan of rapidly boiling salted water until just tender. Drain. Return to pan to keep warm.

3 Drain the oil from the tuna slices, reserving 1 tablespoon. Heat the reserved oil in a large saucepan, add the onion and cook over low heat for 3–4 minutes, or until soft but not brown.

4 Add the garlic and cook for another minute, then add the chopped tomatoes and sugar. Cook over medium heat for 8–10 minutes, or until pulpy.

5 Add the tuna slices, olives and chopped basil, stir well and cook for 2 minutes, or until warmed through.

6 Toss through the spaghetti and season with salt and cracked black pepper. Sprinkle with crumbled feta and serve.

ANGEL HAIR PASTA WITH CREAMY GARLIC PRAWNS

SERVES 4

2 tablespoons olive oil

16 raw prawns, peeled and deveined

1 leek, chopped

6 garlic cloves, crushed

½ teaspoon dried chilli flakes

125 ml (4 fl oz/½ cup) dry white wine

200 ml (7 fl oz) pouring cream

250 g (9 oz) angel hair pasta

3 tablespoons chopped fresh flat-leaf
    (Italian) parsley

1 Heat half the oil in a frying pan, season the prawns with salt and pepper, add to the pan and cook over high heat for 2–3 minutes, or until cooked through. Remove from the pan, cover and keep warm.

2 Heat the remaining oil in the same pan, add the leek and cook, stirring, over medium heat for 2–3 minutes, or until softened.

3 Add the garlic and chilli flakes and stir for 1 minute. Pour in the wine, reduce the heat and simmer for 4 minutes, or until reduced.

4 Add the cream and simmer for 3 minutes, or until just thickened.

5 Meanwhile, cook the pasta in a large pan of rapidly boiling salted water until just tender. Drain and return to the pan to keep warm.

6 Stir the parsley into the sauce and season well. Add to the pasta and stir to coat. Divide the pasta among bowls and top with the prawns.

SPAGHETTI WITH SHELLFISH AND WHITE WINE SAUCE

SERVES 4

500 g (1 lb 2 oz) mussels
1 kg (2 lb 4 oz) clams (vongole)
400 g (13 oz) spaghetti
2 tablespoons olive oil
4 French shallots, finely chopped
2 garlic cloves, crushed
250 ml (9 fl oz/1 cup) dry white wine
3 tablespoons chopped fresh flat-leaf (Italian) parsley

1 Scrub the mussels with a stiff brush and remove any barnacles with a knife. Pull away the beards. Discard any mussels or clams that are broken or open ones that do not close when tapped on the work surface. Wash them both thoroughly under cold running water. Cook the pasta in a large pan of rapidly boiling salted water until just tender. Drain and return to the pan to keep warm.

2 Meanwhile, heat the oil in a large saucepan over medium heat and cook the shallots for 4 minutes, or until softened.

3 Add the garlic and cook for a further 1 minute.

4 Pour in the wine, bring to the boil and cook for 2 minutes, or until reduced slightly.

5 Add the clams and mussels, tossing to coat them in the liquid, then cover the pan. Cook, shaking the pan regularly, for about 3 minutes, or until the shells have opened. Discard any clams or mussels that do not open in the cooking time.

6 Toss the clam mixture through the spaghetti, scatter with parsley and transfer to a warmed serving dish. Season and serve with salad and bread.

SMOKED SALMON PASTA IN CHAMPAGNE SAUCE

SERVES 4

375 g (12 oz) pappardelle

1 tablespoon olive oil

2 large garlic cloves, crushed

125 ml (4 fl oz/½ cup) Champagne

250 ml (9 fl oz/1 cup) thick (double/ heavy) cream

200 g (7 oz) smoked salmon, cut into thin strips

2 tablespoons small capers in brine, rinsed and dried

2 tablespoons snipped chives

2 tablespoons chopped fresh dill

1 Cook the pasta in a large pan of rapidly boiling salted water until just tender. Drain and keep warm.

2 Heat the oil in a frying pan, cook the garlic over a medium heat for 30 seconds. Pour in the Champagne and cook for 2–3 minutes, or until reduced slightly.

3 Add the cream and cook for 3–4 minutes, or until thickened.

4 Toss the sauce and remaining ingredients with the pasta and serve.

PAPPARDELLE WITH LOBSTER AND SAFFRON CREAM SAUCE

SERVES 4

400 g (14 oz) pappardelle

60 g (2¼ oz) butter

4 large garlic cloves, crushed

250 g (9 oz) Swiss brown mushrooms, sliced

500 g (1 lb 2 oz) fresh or frozen lobster tail meat or raw bug tails

125 ml (4 fl oz/½ cup) white wine

½ teaspoon saffron threads

700 ml (24 fl oz) thick (double/heavy) cream

2 egg yolks

1 Cook the pasta in a large pan of rapidly boiling salted water until just tender. Drain. Return to pan to keep warm.

2 Meanwhile, melt the butter in a large deep frying pan, add the garlic and mushrooms and cook over medium heat for 2–3 minutes, or until soft.

3 Add the lobster and cook for 4–5 minutes, or until just cooked through. Remove from the pan.

4 Add the wine and saffron to the pan, scraping the bottom to collect any bits. Bring to the boil and cook for 2–3 minutes, or until reduced.

5 Add the cream, reduce the heat and simmer for 5 minutes.

6 Whisk through the egg yolks until thickened.

7 Return the lobster mixture to the pan and stir until warmed through.

8 Drain the pasta and divide among serving dishes. Spoon on the lobster sauce and season to taste. Serve immediately.

RAVIOLI WITH PRAWNS AND CREAMY LIME SAUCE

SERVES 4

50 g (1¾ oz) butter

4 garlic cloves, crushed

750 g (1 lb 10 oz) medium raw prawns (shrimp), peeled and deveined

1½ tablespoons plain (all-purpose) flour

375 ml (13 fl oz/1½ cups) fish stock

500 ml (17 fl oz/2 cups) pouring (whipping) cream

5 kaffir lime leaves, shredded

650 g (1 lb 7 oz) seafood ravioli (see Note)

3 teaspoons fish sauce

1 **Melt the butter** in a large deep frying pan and cook the garlic over medium heat for 1 minute.

2 **Add the prawns** and cook for 3–4 minutes, or until they turn pink and are cooked through. Remove from the pan, leaving any juices in the pan.

3 **Add the flour** and stir for 1 minute, or until lightly golden. Gradually stir in the stock, then add the cream and lime leaves. Reduce the heat and simmer for 10 minutes, or until slightly thickened.

4 **Meanwhile,** cook the pasta in a large saucepan of boiling salted water until al dente. Drain.

5 **Stir the fish sauce** through the cream sauce, add the prawns and stir until warmed through.

6 **Divide the pasta** among four warm serving plates and spoon on the prawns and sauce. Season with salt and cracked black pepper and serve.

Note: Seafood ravioli is available from speciality pasta shops, but if it is unavailable you can use ricotta ravioli instead — the flavours work well.

FETTUCINE WITH BALSAMIC-SEARED TUNA

SERVES 4

4 x 200 g (7 oz) tuna steaks

170 ml (5½ fl oz/⅔ cup) balsamic vinegar

125 ml (4 fl oz/½ cup) good-quality olive oil

1 lemon

1 clove garlic, finely chopped

1 red onion, finely chopped

2 tablespoons capers, rinsed and dried

½ cup (15 g/½ oz) fresh flat-leaf (Italian) parsley, finely chopped

500 g (1 lb 2 oz) fresh fettucine

1 Place the tuna steaks in a non-metallic dish and cover with the balsamic vinegar. Turn to coat evenly and marinate for 10 minutes.

2 Heat 2 tablespoons of the oil in a large frying pan over medium heat and cook the tuna for 2–3 minutes each side. Remove from the pan, cut into small cubes and transfer to a bowl.

3 Finely grate the zest from the lemon to give ½ teaspoon zest. Squeeze the lemon to give 60 ml (2 fl oz/¼ cup) juice.

4 Wipe the frying pan clean, and heat 2 tablespoons of the olive oil over medium heat, then add the garlic and cook for 30 seconds. Stir in the chopped onion and cook for 2 minutes.

5 Add the lemon zest and capers and cook for 1 minute, then stir in the parsley and cook for 1 minute. Add the lemon juice and remaining oil and gently toss together. Season to taste.

6 Cook the pasta in a large pan of rapidly boiling salted water until just tender. Drain, return to the pan and toss with the caper mixture.

7 Divide the pasta among serving bowls and arrange the tuna pieces over the top.

PASTA WITH ANCHOVIES, BROCCOLI AND BASIL

SERVES 4

600 g (1 lb 5 oz) broccoli, cut into florets

500 g (1 lb 2 oz) orecchiette

1 tablespoon olive oil

4 garlic cloves, finely chopped

8 anchovy fillets, roughly chopped

250 ml (9 fl oz/1 cup) pouring cream

1 very large handful fresh basil, torn

2 teaspoons finely grated lemon zest

100 g (3½ oz) parmesan cheese, grated

1 **Blanch the broccoli** in a large saucepan of boiling salted water for 3–4 minutes. Remove and plunge into chilled water. Drain well with a slotted spoon.

2 **Cook the pasta** in a large pan of rapidly boiling salted water until just tender. Drain and return to the pan to keep warm, reserving 2 tablespoons of the cooking water.

3 **Meanwhile,** heat the oil in a frying pan over medium heat. Add the garlic and anchovies and cook for 1–2 minutes, or until the garlic begins to turn golden.

4 **Add the broccoli** and cook for a further 5 minutes.

5 **Add the cream** and half the basil and cook for 10 minutes, or until the cream has reduced and slightly thickened and the broccoli is very tender.

6 **Purée half the mixture** in a food processor until nearly smooth, then return to the pan with the lemon rind, half the parmesan and 2 tablespoons of the reserved water. Stir together well, then season.

7 **Add the warm pasta** and remaining basil, and toss until well combined. Sprinkle with the remaining parmesan and serve immediately.

CAJUN SCALLOPS WITH PASTA AND BUTTERY CORN

350 g (12 oz) small pasta shells

20 large scallops, without roe

2 tablespoons Cajun spice mix

2 tablespoons corn oil

250 g (9 oz) butter

3 garlic cloves, crushed

400 g (14 oz) can corn kernels, drained

60 ml (2 fl oz/¼ cup) lime juice

4 tablespoons finely chopped fresh coriander (cilantro) leaves

1 Cook the pasta in a large pan of rapidly boiling salted water until just tender. Drain. Return to pan to keep warm.

2 Meanwhile, pat the scallops dry with paper towel and lightly coat in the spice mix.

3 Heat the oil in a large frying pan and cook the scallops for 1 minute each side over high heat (ensuring they are well spaced), then remove from the pan, cover and keep warm.

4 Reduce the heat to medium, add the butter and cook for 4 minutes, or until foaming and golden brown. Remove from the heat, add the garlic, corn and lime juice.

5 Gently toss the corn mixture through the pasta with 2 tablespoons of the coriander and season well.

6 Divide among four serving plates, top with the scallops, drizzle with any juices and sprinkle with the remaining coriander.

Note: Scallops should not be crowded when they are cooked or they will release all their juices, causing them to stew and toughen.

SAFFRON PASTA WITH GARLIC PRAWNS

SERVES 4

125 ml (4 fl oz/½ cup) dry white wine

pinch of saffron threads

500 g (1 lb 2 oz) fresh saffron or plain
angel-hair pasta

1 tablespoon virgin olive oil

30 g (1 oz) butter

750 g (1 lb 10 oz) raw prawns (shrimps),
peeled and deveined

3 garlic cloves, crushed

100 g (3½ oz) butter, for pan-frying,
extra

½ preserved lemon, rinsed, pith and
flesh removed, cut into thin strips

1 tablespoon lemon juice

4 spring onions (scallions), thinly sliced

4 kaffir lime leaves, thinly shredded

125 ml (4 fl oz/½ cup) chicken stock

2 tablespoons snipped chives

1 **Place the wine** and saffron in a small saucepan and boil for 3 minutes, or until reduced by half. Remove from the heat.

2 **Cook the pasta** in a large pan of rapidly boiling salted water until al dente. Drain and return to the pan to keep warm.

3 **Heat the oil** and butter in a large frying pan and cook the prawns in batches over high heat for 3 minutes, or until pink and tender. Cut into thirds, then transfer to a plate and keep warm.

4 **Add the garlic** and extra butter to the same pan and cook over medium heat for 3 minutes, or until golden.

5 **Add the wine** and stir to remove any sediment from the bottom of the pan. Add the preserved lemon, lemon juice, spring onion, lime leaves and stock and bring to the boil, then reduce the heat and simmer for 2 minutes.

6 **Return the prawns** to the frying pan and heat through. Serve the pasta topped with some of the prawns and sauce and sprinkle with chives.

SPAGHETTI WITH OLIVE, CAPER AND ANCHOVY SAUCE

SERVES 4

375 g (13 oz) spaghetti

80 ml (2½ fl oz/⅓ cup) olive oil

2 onions, finely chopped

3 garlic cloves, finely chopped

½ teaspoon chilli flakes

6 large ripe tomatoes, diced

4 tablespoons capers in brine, rinsed, drained

7–8 anchovies in oil, drained, minced

150 g (5½ oz) Kalamata olives

3 tablespoons chopped fresh flat-leaf (Italian) parsley

1   Cook the pasta in a large pan of rapidly boiling salted water until just tender. Drain and return to the pan to keep warm.

2   Meanwhile, heat the oil in a saucepan, add the onion and cook over medium heat for 5 minutes.

3   Add the garlic and chilli flakes, and cook for 30 seconds, then add the tomato, capers and anchovies. Simmer over low heat for 5–10 minutes, or until thick and pulpy, then stir in the olives and parsley.

4   Stir the pasta through the sauce. Season and serve immediately with crusty bread.

SPAGHETTI NIÇOISE

SERVES 4

350 g (12 oz) spaghetti

8 quail eggs (or 4 hen eggs)

3 x 185 g (6½ oz) tins tuna in oil

50 g (1¾ oz/⅓ cup) pitted and halved Kalamata olives

100 g (3½ oz) semi-dried (sun-blushed) tomatoes, halved lengthways

4 anchovy fillets, chopped into small pieces

1 teaspoon finely grated lemon zest

2 tablespoons lemon juice

3 tablespoons baby capers, drained

3 tablespoons chopped fresh flat-leaf (Italian) parsley

1 Cook the pasta in a large saucepan of rapidly boiling salted water until just tender.

2 Meanwhile, place the eggs in a saucepan of cold water, bring to the boil and cook for 4 minutes (10 minutes for hen eggs). Drain, cool under cold water, then peel. Cut the quail eggs into halves or the hen eggs into quarters.

3 Empty the tuna and its oil into a large bowl. Add the olives, tomato halves, anchovies, lemon zest and juice, capers and 2 tablespoons of the parsley.

4 Drain the pasta and rinse in a little cold water, then toss gently through the tuna mixture.

5 Divide among serving bowls, garnish with egg and the remaining chopped fresh parsley, and serve.

LEMON THYME TUNA WITH TAGLIATELLE

SERVES 4

375 g (12 oz) tagliatelle

140 ml extra virgin olive oil

1 small fresh red chilli, seeded and finely chopped

¼ cup (50 g) drained capers

1½ tablespoons fresh lemon thyme leaf tips

500 g tuna steaks, trimmed and cut into 3 cm cubes

¼ cup (60 ml) lemon juice

1 tablespoon grated lemon zest

½ cup (30 g) chopped fresh flat-leaf (Italian) parsley

1 Cook the tagliatelle in a large saucepan of rapidly boiling salted water until just tender. Drain, then return to the pan.

2 Meanwhile, heat 1 tablespoon of the oil in a large frying pan. Add the chilli and capers and cook, stirring, for 1 minute, or until the capers are crisp. Add the thyme and cook for another minute. Transfer to a bowl.

3 Heat another tablespoon of oil in the pan. Add the tuna cubes and toss for 2–3 minutes, or until evenly browned on the outside but still pink in the centre — check with the point of a sharp knife. Remove from the heat.

4 Add the tuna to the caper mixture along with the lemon juice, lemon zest, parsley and the remaining oil, stirring gently until combined.

5 Toss through the pasta, season with freshly ground black pepper and serve immediately.

SMOKED SALMON PASTA

SERVES 4

500 g (1 lb 2 oz) pasta

1 tablespoon olive oil

4 spring onions (scallions), finely
chopped

180 g (6 oz) button mushrooms, sliced

250 ml (9 fl oz/1 cup)) dry white wine

300 ml (10½ fl oz) pouring cream

1 tablespoon finely chopped fresh dill

1 tablespoon lemon juice

90 g (3¼ oz) parmesan cheese, grated

200 g (7 oz) smoked salmon, cut into
strips

shaved parmesan cheese and lemon
wedges, to serve

1 Cook the pasta in a large pan of rapidly boiling salted water until just tender. Drain and return to the pan to keep warm.

2 Meanwhile, heat the oil in a small saucepan, add the spring onion and mushrooms and cook over medium heat for 1–2 minutes, or until soft.

3 Add the wine and cream and bring to the boil, then reduce the heat and simmer for 1 minute.

4 Pour the mushroom sauce over the pasta and stir through the dill and lemon juice. Add the parmesan and stir until warmed through. Remove from the heat and stir in the smoked salmon. Season with pepper and serve with parmesan shavings and lemon wedges.

TAGLIATELLE WITH TUNA, CAPERS AND ROCKET

SERVES 4

3 garlic cloves, crushed

1 teaspoon finely grated lemon zest

4 tablespoons extra virgin olive oil

500 g (1 lb 2 oz) tuna, cut into 1.5 cm (⅝ inch) cubes

350 g (12 oz) fresh tagliatelle

200 g (7 oz) rocket (arugula) leaves, washed, dried and roughly chopped

4 tablespoons baby capers in salt, rinsed and squeezed dry

3 tablespoons lemon juice

2 tablespoons finely chopped flat-leaf (Italian) parsley

1 Combine the garlic, lemon zest and 1 tablespoon of the oil and the tuna in a bowl and season.

2 Meanwhile, cook the pasta in a large saucepan of boiling salted water until just tender. Drain well and return to the pan to keep warm.

3 Heat a non-stick frying pan over high heat. Sear the tuna for 30 seconds on each side. Add the rocket and capers and gently stir for 1 minute, or until the rocket has just wilted. Pour in the lemon juice and then remove from the heat.

4 Add the remaining oil, tuna mixture and parsley to the pasta. Season and toss.

INDEX

GREAT TASTES PASTA

GREAT TASTES PASTA